NOTHIN' BUT
GOOD TIMES
AHEAD
★★★★★★★★★★

G·K
Hall
&Co.

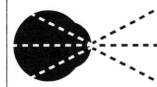

This Large Print Book carries the
Seal of Approval of N.A.V.H.

NOTHIN' BUT GOOD TIMES AHEAD

★★★★★★★★★★

MOLLY IVINS

G.K. Hall & Co.
Thorndike, Maine

Published in 1994 by arrangement with Random House, Inc.

The essays in this work were originally published in *Dallas Times Herald, Fort Worth Star-Telegram, Mother Jones, The Nation, Newsweek, The Progressive,* and *The Texas Observer.*

G.K. Hall Large Print Core Collection.

The text of this Large Print edition is unabridged.
Other aspects of the book may vary from the original edition.

Set in 16 pt. News Plantin.

Printed in the United States on acid-free, high opacity paper. ∞

Library of Congress Cataloging in Publication Data

Ivins, Molly.
  Nothin' but good times ahead / Molly Ivins.
    p.   cm.
  ISBN 0-8161-5925-4 (alk. paper : lg. print)
  1. United States — Politics and government — 1993 - — Humor.
  2. United States — Politics and government — 1989 - 1993 — Humor.
  3. Presidents — United States — Election — 1992 — Humor.
  4. Large type books. I. Title.
  [E885.I95   1994]
  973.929'0207—dc20   93-43545

To my father, Jim Ivins,
who taught me to love books,
and
To my mother, Margot Milne Ivins,
who taught me to love laughter

PREFACE

AUSTIN, TEXAS — I was goin' along all right there — just your fairly normal human political reporter — when I accidentally became a best-selling author. This will complicate your life. In fact, it frequently causes a level of confusion worthy of Admiral James Stockdale.

When a girl like I (Janet Reno is my Fashion Goddess) becomes conversant with such exotic television concepts as eyebrow mousse, the cultural confusion is almost as awful as a redistricting fight in the Texas Legislature. But I have done my best to soldier on, aided by a political landscape so deliciously wacky that not even the vicissitudes of bein' an arthur — as we still say in East Texas — can distract one for long.

The best description I ever found of what it's like to be a political reporter was printed, curiously enough, in *Natural History* magazine, deftly sandwiched into an article by a woman biologist who studies the diet of the muriqui monkey. Anyone who has ever chased a politician around trying to get a usable quote will be stunned by the extraordinary accuracy of this scientific account of the procedure:

"While simple in theory, my role in these investigations has not been easy. The biochemical analyses of the plant foods require gathering a grocery bag full of leaves or fruit from each plant species, and doing this after the muriquis have swarmed through one of their feeding trees is not as simple as it sounds. Collecting fresh fecal samples from identified individuals is equally laborious. The feces themselves are not so unpleasant to collect as one might suppose because they carry an aromatic scent from the cinnamon leaves that muriquis consume. The challenge, rather, is to get almost directly underneath the targeted individual at the moment of defecation so that the greenish brown dung can be spotted before it is camouflaged after hitting the ground.

"Occasionally the feces land neatly in my glove, but more often they splatter uselessly in the tangled vegetation — or else fall alongside another muriqui's feces, so that I cannot tell whose is whose. So even though the muriquis defecate often and, in the case of adults, abundantly each time, getting a clean sample sometimes means tailing one muriqui for up to six hours without pause."

My pursuit of this delicate trade kept getting interrupted by the odd jobs that fall to the arthur in our time. At one point in the blooming middle of the presidential campaign, I had to leave Little Rock and fly to New York to appear at a literary tea for *Newsday*.

I dutifully flew to New York, and I dutifully reported to the Waldorf-Astoria, where sure as a by-God there were 350 blue-haired ladies having tea. I met my fellow arthurs. We were: Elmore Leonard, who writes the great murder mysteries out of Detroit City (I've met him twice now, so I call him "Dutch"); Professor Henry Gates of Harvard University, a black intellectual and a very hot ticket on the multicultural circuit; and . . . Ivana Trump. Ivana, as she asked us to call her, paid somebody to write a really bad novel for her, which I point out in her defense is still better than Marilyn Quayle's novel.

After Leonard, Gates, and I had held forth on *la vie littéraire* from our several perspectives, Ivana addressed the blue-hairs with her wonderful Czech accent. She told them she luffs ze literary life; forr herr, reading her book iss like looking in ze mirror, Katrina in ze book iss like her seester. (It's a wretched roman à clef about The Donald.) In addition to ze literary work, said Ivana, herr life iss verry busy. She hass ze shildren. She hass ze sharities. Also, she iss bringing out a new line of toiletries.

At that point I lost it and had to hide my face in a plateful of tea sandwiches. When I recovered, I told Dutch Leonard we should both can the writing gig: He can bring out Eau de Detroit Funk, A Cologne for Men, I'll bring out Molly Ivins's Barbecue-Flavored Vaginal Gel, and we'll both get rich in toiletries, screw the arthur bidness. Then I went back to being a political writer. Given the way the '92 race shaped up, I should have stuck to toiletries.

Oh yeah, while all this other stuff was happening, I also became broke and unemployed for several months. Happily for my life and work, I managed to remain rooted in Texas through it all, which always gives one the refreshing perspective that the lunatic is normal. This dog's breakfast of a collection is the result.

Fellow citizens, as we stagger toward the millenium, I can only hope that this modest oeuvre — as we often say in Amarillo — will remind you that we need to stop and laugh along the way. We live in a Great Nation, but those who attempt to struggle through it unarmed with a sense of humor are apt to wind up in my Aunt Eula's Fort Worth Home for the Terminally Literal-Minded, gibbering like some demented neoconservative about the Decline of Civilization.

Any nation that can survive what we have lately in the way of government is on the high road to permanent glory. So hang in there, keep fightin' for freedom, raise more hell, and don't forget to laugh, too.

Yours in the belief that the Founders were right all along, but that the results are a lot funnier than they intended.

Molly Ivins
August 1993

ACKNOWLEDGMENTS

The person who deserves the credit not just for this book but for saving my life is Elizabeth Peake Faulk, peerless personal assistant/secretary/manager, and the most wonderful, sensible friend anyone could have. Liz's famous practicality included noticing that I would shortly drop dead if I didn't get some help in the first place. A thousand times thank you.

Thanks also to Mike Blackman and Ken Bunting of the *Fort Worth Star-Telegram* for hiring me, for letting me write, and for taking the flak that followed. Thanks also to my colleagues in the *Star-Telegram*'s Austin bureau, especially ol' Scoop Cutbirth, for putting up with the phone calls and answering several thousand dumb questions.

My thanks to my friend Marlyn Schwartz, without whom I could not have survived the book tour; and to all the Usual Suspects, including Eden Lipson, Ida and Jesse Frankel, the Friday night gang at Zona Rosa, the river runners, the Albach Hilton, and all the pals whose support and common sense saved my sanity. It wasn't fear of success that bothered me, just fear of becoming an asshole; and that was no fear at all with friends like these.

Thanks again to my agent, Dan Green, who un-

derstands that I do not believe in income max-
imization, and to Peter Osnos and the great gang
at Random House.

And to my beloved targets in public life; how
could I miss with material this good? Keep it up.
Maybe we'll save the Republic by accident.

I AM THE COSMOS

"So write about Camille Paglia," suggested the editor. Like any normal person, I replied, "And who the hell might she be?"

Big cheese in New York intellectual circles. The latest rage. Hot stuff. Controversial.

But I'm not good on New York intellectual controversies, I explained. Could never bring myself to give a rat's ass about Jerzy Kosinski. Never read Andy Warhol's diaries. Can never remember the name of the editor of this *New Whatsit*, the neo-con critical rag. I'm a no-hoper on this stuff, practically a professional provincial.

Read Paglia, says he, you'll have an opinion. So I did; and I do.

Christ! Get this woman a Valium!

Hand her a gin. Try meditation. Camille, honey, calm down!

The noise is about her oeuvre, as we always say in Lubbock: *Sexual Personae: Art and Decadence from Nefertiti to Emily Dickinson*. In very brief, for those of you who have been playing hooky from *The New York Review of Books*, Ms. Paglia's contention is that "the history of western civilization has been a constant struggle between . . . two impulses, an unending tennis match between cold, Apollonian categorization and Dionysian lust and chaos." Jeez, me too. I always thought the world was divided into only two kinds of people — those who think the world is divided into only two kinds of people, and those who don't.

You think perhaps this is a cheap shot, that I have searched her work and caught Ms. Paglia in a rare moment of sweeping generalization, easy to make fun of? *Au contraire,* as we always say in Amarillo; the sweeping generalization is her signature. In fact, her work consists of damn little else. She is the queen of the categorical statement.

Never one to dodge a simple dichotomy when she can set one up, Ms. Paglia holds that the entire error of Western civilization stems from denying that nature is a kind of nasty, funky, violent wet dream, and that Judeo-Christianity has been one long effort to ignore this. She pegs poor old Rousseau, that fathead, as the initiator of the silly notion that Nature is benign and glorious and that only civilization corrupts.

Right away, I got a problem. Happens I have spent a lot of my life in the wilderness, and also a lot of my life in bars. When I want sex and violence, I go to a Texas honky-tonk. When I want peace and quiet, I head for the woods. Just as a minor historical correction to Ms. Paglia, Rousseau did not invent the concept of benign Nature. Among the first writers to advance the theory that nature was a more salubrious environment for man

14

than the corruptions of civilization were the Roman Stoics — rather a clear-eyed lot, I always thought.

Now, why, you naturally ask, would anyone care about whether a reviewer has ever done any serious camping? Ah, but you do not yet know the Camille Paglia school of I-am-the-cosmos argument. Ms. Paglia believes that all her personal experiences are Seminal. Indeed, Definitive. She credits a large part of her supposed wisdom to having been born post–World War II and thus having been raised on television. Damn me, so was I.

In addition to the intrinsic cultural superiority Ms. Paglia attributes to herself from having grown up watching television (*Howdy Doody* obviously made us all smarter), she also considers her own taste in music to be of enormous significance. "From the moment the feminist movement was born, it descended into dogma," she told an interviewer for *New York* magazine. "They stifled any kind of debate, any kind of dissent. Okay, it's Yale, it's New Haven in '69, I am a rock fanatic, okay. . . . So I was talking about taste to these female rock musicians, and I said the Rolling Stones were the greatest rock band, and that just set them off. They said, 'The Rolling Stones are sexist, and it's bad music because it's sexist.' I said: 'Wait a minute. You can't make judgments about art on the basis of whether it fits into some dogma.' And now they're yelling, screaming, saying that nothing that demeans women can be art.

"You see, right from the start it was impossible

15

for me to be taken into the feminist movement, okay? The only art they will permit is art that gives a positive image of women. I said, 'That's like the Soviet Union; that is the demagogic, propagandistic view of art.' "

Well, by George, as a First Amendment absolutist, you'll find me willing to spring to the defense of Camille Paglia's right to be a feminist Rolling Stones fan any hour, day or night. Come to think of it, who the hell was the Stalin who wouldn't let her do that? I went back and researched the '69 politburo, and all I could find was Betty Friedan, Bella Abzug, and Gloria Steinem, none of whom ever seems to have come out against rock music.

I have myself quite cheerfully been both a country-music fan and a feminist for years — if Camille Paglia is the cosmos, so am I. When some fellow feminist doesn't like my music (How could you not like "You are just another sticky wheel on the grocery cart of life"?), I have always felt free to say, in my politically correct feminist fashion, "Fuck off."

In a conversation printed in *Harper's* magazine, Paglia held forth on one of her favorite themes — Madonna, the pop singer: "The latest atavistic discoverer of the pagan heart of Catholicism is Madonna. This is what she's up to. She doesn't completely understand it herself. When she goes on *Nightline* and makes speeches about celebrating the body, as if she's some sort of Woodstock hippie, she's way off. She needs

16

me to tell her." I doubt that.

Bram Dijkstra, author of a much-praised book, *Idols of Perversity*, which is a sort of mirror image of *Sexual Personae*, said that Paglia "literally drags the whole nineteenth-century ideological structure back into the late eighteenth century, really completely unchanged. What's so amazing is that she takes all that nineteenth-century stuff, Darwinism and social Darwinism, and she reasserts it and reaffirms it in this incredibly dualistic fashion. In any situation, she establishes the lowest common denominator of a point. She says, 'This is the feminist point of view,' and overturns it by standing it on its head. She doesn't go outside what she critiques; she simply puts out the opposite of it.

"For example," Dijkstra continues, "she claims, 'Feminism blames rape on pornography,' which is truly the reductio ad absurdum of the feminist point of view. Of course there are very many feminist points of view, but then she blows away this extremely simplified opposite, and we are supposed to consider this erudition. She writes aphorisms and then throws them out, one after the other, so rapid-fire the reader is exhausted."

Tracing Paglia's intellectual ancestry is a telling exercise; she's the lineal descendant of Ayn Rand, who in turn was a student of William Graham Sumner, one of the early American sociologists and an enormously successful popularizer of social Darwinism. Sumner was in turn a disciple of Herbert Spencer, that splendid nineteenth-century kook. Because Paglia reasserts ideas so ingrained in our thinking, she has become popular by re-affirming common prejudices.

Paglia's obsession with de Sade is beyond my competence, although the glorification of sadomasochism can easily be read as a rationalization of bondage into imagined power, a characteristic process of masochistic transfer. Dijkstra suggests that the Sadean notion of the executioner's assistant is critical to her thinking, though one wonders if there is not also some identification with de Sade the Catholic aristocrat.

Paglia's view of sex — that it is irrational, violent, immoral, and wounding — is so glum that one hesitates to suggest that it might be instead, well, a lot of fun, and maybe even affectionate and loving.

Far less forgivable is Paglia's consistent confusion of feminism with yuppies. What *does* she think she's doing? Paglia holds feminists responsible for the bizarre blight created by John T. Molloy, author of *Dress for Success*, which caused a blessedly brief crop of young women, all apparently aspiring to be executive vice presidents, to appear in the corporate halls wearing those awful sand-colored baggy suits with little floppy bow ties around their necks.

Why Paglia lays the blame for this at the feet of feminism is beyond me. Whatever our other aims may have been, no one in the feminist movement ever thought you are what you wear. The only coherent fashion statement I can recall from the entire movement was the suggestion that Mrs.

Cleaver, Beaver's mom, would on the whole have been a happier woman had she not persisted in vacuuming while wearing high heels. This, I still believe.

In an even more hilarious leap, Paglia contends that feminism is responsible for the aerobics craze and concern over thin thighs. Speaking as a beer-drinking feminist whose idea of watching her diet is to choose the baked potato either with sour cream or with butter, but not with both, I find this loony beyond all hope — and I am the cosmos, too.

What we have here, fellow citizens, is a crassly egocentric, raving twit. The Norman Podhoretz of our gender. That this woman is actually taken seriously as a thinker in New York intellectual circles is a clear sign of decadence, decay, and hopeless pinheadedness. Has no one in the nation's intellectual capital the background and ability to see through a web of categorical assertions? One fashionable line of response to Paglia is to claim that even though she may be fundamentally off-base, she has "flashes of brilliance." If so, I missed them in her oceans of swill.

One of her latest efforts at playing enfant terrible in intellectual circles was a peppy essay for *Newsday*, claiming that either there is no such thing as date rape or, if there is, it's women's fault because we dress so provocatively. Thanks, Camille, I've got some Texas fraternity boys I want you to meet.

There is one area in which I think Paglia and

I would agree that politically correct feminism has produced a noticeable inequity. Nowadays, when a woman behaves in a hysterical and disagreeable fashion, we say, "Poor dear, it's probably PMS." Whereas, if a man behaves in a hysterical and disagreeable fashion, we say, "What an asshole." Let me leap to correct this unfairness by saying of Paglia, Sheesh, what an asshole.

Mother Jones, October 1991

THE THING THING

Consider George Bush. I know, it's an unappetizing prospect, but do it anyway, just for the exercise. The man has been president for three years now, our elected monarch. Such is the system we've had in this country since 1987, when it became clear that the Constitution was so much confetti to the Reagan administration.

After eight years of Reagan, Bush initially looked like a better bet, considering the constraints of comparison shopping. He seemed brighter than Reagan and could stay awake through entire meetings. But familiarity has not made his personality more comprehensible.

Would any other grown man who has served in the United States Navy use the word *darn* naturally? Why does he do it? The guy must think the American people are the Tennessee fainting goats of the human race — someone says "damn," and we all flop over on our backs with our feet pointing in the air, out cold, up to fifty times a day.

The psycholinguistics people are going to have to help us understand the way Bush uses language.

His thing thing is actually getting worse, and the cause of his aversion to verbs remains an utter mystery. "*Sadd*-em . . . Kuwait . . . world . . . out," was Bush's most definitive explanation of why we went to war.

We need expert help on his body-language tics, too. Have you noticed that he gets many of his gestures backward? While Bush is saying, "This deficit thing is getting bigger and bigger," his hand goes toward the floor. Once, as he was saying, "I want to bring people together," I noticed that his hands went flying out in the gesture for breaking apart. Is this a rare form of dyslexia?

Turns out the experts have been pondering these very problems, and they do not bring us good news. Professor Robin Lakoff of the University of California has written a book called *Talking Power*, in which she analyzes Bush's speech style and concludes that it is profoundly "feminine." Great. Wouldn't you know they'd find some way to blame women for all this? Give us a break, O great experts: Did Barbara Jordan ever sound like a ditz? All of us going through school had some Miss Dove or Miss Witherspoon — did she ever sound as whiny as Bush does? Margaret Thatcher may have had her limitations, but at least she never referred to trouble as "deep doo-doo."

Discussing her theory in an interview with the *East Bay Express*, Lakoff said: "People who don't know who they are, or are afraid of who they are, are the people who should make us the most nervous. What is striking about Bush is that he has no real center. . . . Bush's speaking style [is] not so much that of women, as of someone without power, although it comes to the same thing. It's the language of someone who needs approval above all, which is frequently true of women. . . .

"[Bush used to] gesture an unusual amount, particularly for a New England WASP. And the gestures he made were especially feminine — fluttery gestures, doing funny hula-dancer moves with his fingers. He often was photographed with his hands on his hips, something men are allowed to do, but atypical."

Lakoff believes that Bush's advisers have tried to change the president's gestures to more stereotypically masculine gesticulations. Now he points, makes fists, and squares frames with his hands. "The impression Bush gives through his speaking style is of a man who's barely in control. . . . It's probably a combination of nervousness and not quite knowing how to be the kind of guy he wants to be. By the use of the particular idioms and metaphors he selects, he's trying to project himself as George Bush, the western he-man. But because he isn't . . . he can only approximate it. So he's a preppy western he-man."

Lakoff's interviewer quoted Dana Carvey, who impersonates Bush on *Saturday Night Live*. Bush is easy for impressionists: You just do Mr. Rogers doing John Wayne.

George Bush's speech patterns can upset almost anyone. The normally mild-mannered Tom

Wicker got teed off not long ago: "Mr. Bush not only seemed wounded by the obtuse world he sees out there; he indulged himself in Bushspeak, a language — or something — a local alderman might not dignify with use."

The hyperkinetic approach that Bush takes to both body language and the English language extends to his overall manner, as well. Hugh Liedtke, who was George Bush's partner in the oil bidness back in Midland, Texas, and according to oil-patch lore, the one with the brains who made both of them rich, was interviewed on a C-SPAN program not long ago. They asked him if George Bush was still the same guy he had partnered with all those years ago. Sure he is, said Liedtke. "He was always *doing* something back then and he's always *doing* something now."

And so he is, tearing around playing golf or horseshoes or rushing off hither and thither. George Bush has already traveled abroad more in his first two and a half years as president than any of his predecessors ever managed. George Will has described him as "frenetic." Upon learning that he had a thyroid condition, I thought, Aha, that explains it.

We have all long since resigned ourselves to the realization that Bush is no Winston Churchill. Given recent events, it would be unfair to suggest that Pee-wee Herman is closer to the role model he presents. Personally, I think Eddie Haskell from *Leave it to Beaver* is the man. This came to me as I was reading a description of Bush on the golf

24

course, missing a putt. "Shoo-oot! Golly! Darn!" said our leader. Face it, if Eddie had grown up and become president, he'd sound exactly like George Bush.

Mother Jones, November/December 1991

THE DIPLOMATS — NOT THE SOLDIERS — GOT US INTO THIS MESS

Every day it becomes more surreal. There you are half-watching a football game when a voice cries, "Let's go! Let's go! It's a Patriot, let's go!" Strange, aren't we watching the Raiders and the Bills? Well, let's thank the Raiders for their remarkable restraint in failing to retaliate whenever the Bills scored a touchdown.

Odd thoughts keep creeping in during those long discussions with the maps and the pointers and the charts — what *are* we doing defending a country that doesn't let women drive? Rank cultural chauvinism, of course. Why do we keep expecting the rest of the world to be like us?

The crowds gather and chant "USA! USA!" as though it were a hockey game. The jingoism kicks in. "Well," said a student in Washington, "I was against getting into this war, but now we have to support them. It would be unpatriotic not to." That old, simpleminded equation.

If you think the war was neither necessary nor

wise and you doubt much good will come out of it, that means you're against Our Boys and Girls who are, God bless them, putting their lives on the line so we can sit on our butts and watch it all on TV.

As though many of us haven't a special reason to cringe every time we hear we've lost another plane. As though losing someone you loved in Vietnam weren't enough to teach you forever to make the distinction between the soldiers who fight the war and the fools who get us into it. The soldiers who fight for our country are not responsible for the mistakes of diplomats and leaders.

I believe that Americans not only have an obligation to support the troops in the Gulf, we also have an obligation to learn how we got into this and just what complexities we face in the Middle East. If you're not up to any of the several excellent books on the topic (Tom Friedman's *From Beirut to Jerusalem*, for example) try Chris Hitchens's article in the January issue of *Harper's* magazine. It's a wonder to me American diplomats can bring themselves to speak with a straight face about the suffering of the Kurds under Saddam Hussein.

Speaking of past mistakes, my favorite item in the transcript of the meeting between Saddam and the American ambassador to Iraq April Glaspie last July 25, just before Saddam invaded Kuwait, is this little conversational tidbit: Glaspie to Saddam, "We have no opinion on the Arab-Arab conflicts, like your border disagreement with Kuwait. I was in the American embassy in Kuwait in the late '60s. The instruction we had during this period was that we should express no opinion on this issue, and that the issue is not associated with America. James Baker has directed our official spokesman to emphasize this instruction."

Actually, the most ghastly moment in that conversation, in retrospect, is when Glaspie confided to Saddam, "We have many Americans who would like to see the price go to about $25 [a barrel] because they come from oil-producing states."

But some of our mistakes still lie in the future. After all the bodies are buried and all the tears have been shed, here's a little number that will still be with us: BUSH WON'T PUSH TAX HIKE TO FINANCE WAR. First time the government has not raised taxes to help finance a war. But during Vietnam, they waited so long to put on a surtax the inflation lasted for ten years.

The estimated cost of this war is now between under $500 million and $1 billion per day. Look on the bright side: Even if the high estimate is correct, we can still fight for almost two years before this war costs us as much as the S&L bailout. (First guy who thinks of Neil Bush gets called a Saddam-symp.)

Since this has all been such a bizarre television show, I am seized with a vision of an announcer calling. "George Bush. COME OOON DOWN! George Bush, this is your chance of a lifetime. You get to go on an unlimited spending spree — $1 billion a day until the money runs out. Now, George Bush, what will you do with your money?"

Sooner or later, someone is bound to point out that we could have bought Kuwait back for the price.

It was all rather fun, wasn't it, until they showed the captured pilots on (where else) TV, those poor men, barely able to hold their heads up, having to speak utter swill. Suddenly, there you are, thinking viciously, "Damn them, damn them."

It's a dandy little war for paranoia too. First we have air superiority, then more Scuds arrive, and they still have seven hundred planes. Either the military is lying to us or they don't know anything. Just when your skepticism level is pushed beyond the breaking point — how many Scuds can hit Tel Aviv and Riyadh before they'll admit someone got killed — someone gets killed and you wish we could go back to pretending it doesn't happen.

Dallas Times Herald, January 27, 1991

WE SHOULDN'T HAVE BEEN SURPRISED BY IRAQ'S REFUSAL TO FIGHT

"And, by God, we're over the Vietnam syndrome at last!"
— last sentence of George Bush's address to state legislators at the White House, March 2

Hard to know whether to be more relieved than appalled at the events of the last week. As one who approached the thought of a ground war with visions of The Wall dancing in my head, a Persian Gulf Memorial with tens of thousands of new American names on it, I was so relieved at the low casualty rate I almost promised to give up Baptist sin on the spot, and divided my time between thanking God and thanking General Schwarzkopf.

I notice it is now fashionable to blame the press for what turned out to be wild overestimates of the American casualties involved in this endeavor. All the press did was quote the estimates made by American military experts, which ranged from twenty thousand to forty thousand in the mainstream and higher and lower estimates by those regarded as on the extremes.

The lowest I heard was Representative Les Aspin's memorable "merely a few thousand." So now the press gets blamed for spreading misinformation. Oh, well.

The one guy who turned out to be on the money concerning Iraq's military capabilities is Edward Said, the Arabist, who was denounced as some kind of leftist nut early on in the crisis when he claimed they had been "fantastically exaggerated."

On the other hand, I am still stunned by everyone else's surprise that the Iraqis wouldn't fight. They had already surrendered when George Bush started the ground war. I thought when the guy yelled "Uncle!" you were supposed to stop hitting him.

The Iraqis tried and tried to surrender, and Bush just would not take yes for an answer.

Here are all these military analysts on television solemnly announcing, "They lacked the key element, the will to fight, they did not believe in their cause."

No kidding, Sherlock. The Iraqis were trying to get out before we came in. We had offered them one week. They had asked for three weeks.

The Soviets said they could talk the Iraqis down to a week and then Bush gave them twenty-four hours. Presto, ground war.

When you've won, you've won, enough already.

According to the Saudis, we killed between 85,000 and 100,000 Iraqis in four days of nonwar.

(American estimates are between 25,000 and 50,000. I'm working on a new theory of military math based on our experience in this war. You notice the original report of atrocities in Kuwait City claimed the Iraqis had rounded up and marched off 40,000 Kuwaiti hostages. This was later lowered to 4,000. So deduce that what we should do is divide all casualty estimates by ten, and multiply all cost estimates of new weapons systems by the same number, as per earlier experience.)

The one unmitigated good to come out of this adventure was the liberation of Kuwait, a genuinely joyous and thrilling event. But as I have pointed out, this was a policy war, the result of deliberate policies over a period of years, and it is already clear we haven't learned a damn thing from it.

What to our wondering eyes should appear, in midrout, but some burbling television commentator taking note of what our allies are getting out of this war: in the case of Hafez al-Assad of Syria, $2 billion.

"I'll bet he's about to go on a shopping spree," said the commentator. Assad, you recall, is the one who can, on a good day, make Saddam Hussein look like a Boy Scout. Assad is the man responsible for the expression Hama Rules, meaning no rules at all (killed twenty thousand of his own people in the city of Hama in 1983).

To this charmer we have just presented $2 billion so he can build up *his* store of chemical, biological, and nuclear weapons.

Also excelling on the logic front was the British foreign minister, who told President Bush we should continue the economic sanctions on Iraq "in order to assure that Iraq pays reparations." Think that one through.

As a principle of justice, reparations are an attractive, nonviolent means of settling international scores. But as a practical matter, they often don't work out, as we learned from Germany after World War I.

Iraq has just been destroyed. Demanding that it pay reparations to Kuwait, one of the richest countries in the world, at this point makes no sense.

Here's why we all like General Schwarzkopf, with his charts and pointers, so much. It came to me when he was explaining the Hail Mary pass and the flanking movements: He's coach John Madden with a haircut, circles and arrows and all.

A new low on the football analogy front: A San Antonio radio talk-show host referred to the noon deadline last Saturday as "kickoff time."

Much patriotic gore still to be waded through in coming days, and I expect there are more horror stories to come. But as Obi Wan Kenobi said: "Luke, don't give in to hate. That leads to the dark side."

Dallas Times Herald, March 3, 1991

PRINCIPLES, NOT OPPORTUNISM, INSPIRED TOWER'S POLITICS

A cynical friend, upon hearing me express distress over the death of John Tower, and knowing how seldom we had ever agreed on matters political, said, "Oh, yeah, name me one good thing about John Tower."

"He was never mean about race," I replied, and then realized it sounded as though I were damning with faint praise. In fact, that was the core of the early John Tower — he was a civilized man whose conservatism stemmed from thought and principle, not from racism or meanness or opportunism. He was first elected with the help and support of Texas liberals — the Democratic candidate that year was an unbelievable dog — and 1961 was a time when race baiting was still acceptable in this state and would have helped get him elected. But he never played that game for political advantage.

My parents, who knew him better in the early days than I did, recall him as a young professor from Wichita Falls who genuinely excited and encouraged his students and who had, in addition, an endearing twinkle in his eye, a mildly mischievous and ironic appreciation for the absurdities of both our state and of politics.

That made him a most unusual conservative at a time when Texas Republican politics were dominated by true-believer Goldwaterites and John Birchers who could never discuss politics without getting all red in the face and having the veins in their necks pop out, they would get so angry. They used to remind me of irate turkey gobblers. Tower, more of an intellectual than a true believer, enjoyed discussing political and economic theory and did so with intelligence and charm.

He never seemed to suffer from that sense of intellectual inferiority that so plagued Lyndon Johnson, from having gone to a small Texas college rather than Harvard or Yale. In addition to his graduate work at the University of London and Southern Methodist University, I suspect Tower got quite a good education at Southwestern University in Georgetown, a Methodist school. Texans used to do that — become well educated at small church schools no one ever heard of.

I don't know what happened to John Tower in Washington. I never covered him there. I did one investigative piece at the end of his second term and found practically nothing in his record — a dull, respectable, extremely conservative record. He was doing what one was supposed to do in Washington then (and now): sitting there quietly accumulating seniority until he could become a major player.

There was a school of thought among the rather stuffy, country-club Republicans that he should never have divorced his first wife, that all his problems stemmed from letting that nice lady go. We heard that he drank; there was a rather famous occasion in which he passed out in the chili at his annual Texas Independence Day party (amazing that anyone there was sober enough to remember).

I suspect that's all there ever was to the corruption of John Tower — he just did what everybody else did. Everybody drank too much, especially if they were divorced and lonely. And no increasingly powerful United States senator has ever remained lonely long. (All that sexual freedom must have been heady indeed to a Methodist boy from Texas.) Everybody took money from PACs. Everybody took leftover "campaign funds" with them when they left office. His second marriage was notoriously rocky and ended in a nasty divorce — one more good reason to drink.

By then, there was apparently little left of the early idealism. The 1984 *Almanac of American Politics* says flatly, "Tower is not courtly, nor particularly congenial. He does not suffer fools. He does not sway other senators by charm or humor. However, he is effective, because he is brainy, usually well prepared, and always ready to take maximum advantage of circumstances. And he is nobody's patsy."

On his long-desired position as chairman of the Senate Armed Services Committee: "His own views are unambiguous; he supports defense spending increases, the larger the better; he tends to back Pentagon decisions, though not mechanically. . . . He runs a tight ship."

He wanted terribly to be secretary of defense, and his rejection was a searing, scarring experience for him. Don't read his book on the subject. It's too bitter, too defensive, too sad, too ugly. And in an odd way, too right. What he argues again and again, in text and subtext, is that he never did anything more than everybody else did.

When corruption becomes the norm, no one recognizes it as corruption. John Tower went to a Washington awash in special interests; he played the game, just like everybody else. He became arrogant, in part because of the endless flattery powerful people receive there, in part because he was smarter than most of them and tactless enough, or honest enough, to let it show. So they brought him down. Rather Greek, all that; hubris and such.

The last tragedy strikes me as by far the worst: that his daughter died with him. Whatever his failings and stupidities concerning other women, he did dearly love his daughters. He would have given his life to have prevented that.

Dallas Times Herald, April 6, 1991

WHERE IS THE JUSTICE IN ENORMOUS DISPARITY IN SENTENCES?

Two truly horrific pieces of news arrived simultaneously last week, causing the sort of deep funk that moves all right-thinkers to repair to the nearest bar or to crawl under the bed and eat chocolate-covered Oreos. There will soon be 1 million lawyers in this country — it resonates, doesn't it? Also, Phil Gramm is about to appoint fourteen new federal judges in the state of Texas. As they say in the comics, "AIEEEEEEE!"

The idea of fourteen new federal judges appointed by Phil Gramm naturally brings to mind the "conservative" jurists we already have. Judge Joe Fish of Dallas has been getting a lot of flak lately for being squishy soft on white-collar crime.

Several citizens were upset that Don Dixon, late of the Vernon Savings and Loan Association and perhaps the most notorious of that entire crew, was sentenced by Judge Fish to a mere five years in some federal playpen, a stretch sure to be halved by good time. This does seem fairly easy cheese, given that Dixon's Guy Friday Woody Lemons got thirty years for doing what Dixon told him to do.

Fish drew fire earlier for sentencing socialite Carol Peeler to one thousand hours of community service because of her splendid record with the Junior League. Ms. Peeler, you may recall, was accused of tax fraud that cost the U.S. Treasury $750 million. Her colleague John T. "Corky" Jaeger, who was never in the Junior League but is a former son-in-law of Mayor Annette Strauss, got three years' probation from Judge Fish.

All they did was help hundreds of well-heeled Americans dodge millions of dollars in income taxes by selling them phony tax losses on non-existent securities. But I'm sure all those rich tax dodgers wore yellow ribbons during the Persian Gulf war. The affable Judge Fish had previously demonstrated his notion of getting tough on crime by giving Ed Cox, Jr. (fraudulent loans of $80 million), six months in a federal pen of his choice.

But, my friends, there is always another side to the story, and lest you think Judge Fish is unduly lenient on white-collar crime, let me point out what happens in his court to those who are not rich, white, and socially prominent. Regard, if you will, the fate of Shirley Harris, no kin to the mayor, not in the Junior League, and an Okie on top of it.

Harris, along with her husband, her brother, and five others, was indicted for conspiracy, wire fraud, and mail fraud in connection with another

Dallas-based cosmetics-franchising business. Raphael Cosmetics accepted franchise fees averaging $8,400 from at least forty folks around the country and then didn't make good on its promise to turn the franchises into lucrative small businesses. Shirley Harris, a Piedmont, Oklahoma, housewife, opened the Dallas office and answered the phones there during the short life of Raphael Cosmetics.

She told the judge she had not known what her husband and her brother was doing was criminal and that she was afraid of her abusive husband. Judge Fish, proving to us all how tough he is on crime, gave Shirley Harris a sixty-year prison sentence.

That's only ten times as long as the average sentence for mail fraud and four times as long as the previous record sentence for that offense.

Five for Don Dixon, sixty for Shirley Harris. Makes sense to me.

She should've tried harder to get into the Junior League. And probably would have, if she hadn't been raped when she was fourteen, forced to bear an illegitimate child at a home for unwed mothers, and then married an abusive man.

Hey, luck that bad, no wonder she got Joe Fish for a judge.

Fourteen new Joe Fishes on the bench.

Dallas Times Herald, April 7, 1991

CAPITALIZING ON THE QUEEN'S VISIT TO THIS HERE FINE STATE

We would be getting into a total tizzy here in the state capital over the forthcoming visit of the queen of England, if only we could stop laughing long enough. No one seems to have any idea why this poor woman is coming to visit: It's not as though anyone had asked her.

My suspicion is that Prince Charles, after his dynamic visitation here in 1986 for our double-jump-up, jim-dandy Sesquicentennial, went home and told the queen: "Jeez, Mom, you have gotta go to Texas. You will not believe that place."

You may recall that Prince Charles, a most urbane and sophisticated man, who is quite accustomed to the sight of assorted natives leaping about in loincloths in an effort to entertain him, seemed slightly stunned by the members of the Texas Legislature, dressed in their best polyester Western wear, who came up to shake his hand, saying, "Hidy, Prince Chuck." Hey, me no Alamo. It was our only Speaker, Ol' Under-Indictment-

41

Again Gib Lewis, who greeted the prince during the special session in his honor by saying, "Ah cain't tell yew how happy yew are to be here."

I thought the prince was going to lose it entirely when we made him cut the Sesquicentennial cake, which was larger than a basketball court and made from our famous old state recipe, the Duncan Hines Yellow Mix. He used his sword to cut the thing.

So anyway, we're all brushing up on our royal etiquette again for the queen. There's a list circulating in the capitol of surefire conversation starters with her, such as, "Yo, Queenie, so what's in your purse?" And, "Didn't you wear that hat last year?"

I haven't followed this closely, but someone told me we are making a major effort not to flash our collective posterior at the queen, so she's being taken to a lot of boring, genteel stuff like symphonies.

Hell, they have symphonies in London. I say we just lay it out there and show her why we're different. Bring on the Kilgore Rangerettes, the Dallas Cowboy Cheerleaders, the Aggie band, a rattlesnake round-up, Speaker Lewis and the entire Legislature, the Cotton-Eyed Joe, a couple of feedlots, three rodeos, four honky-tonks, and a partridge in a pear tree. Remember the state motto: Too Much Is Not Enough, and Wretched Excess Is Even More Fun.

Dallas Times Herald, May 19, 1991

THE QUEEN AND
THE REUNION — A VEDDY
INTERESTING CONTRAST

It was two A.M. at the Jiffy Mart, and the lady behind the counter interrupted her conversation with the other lady behind the counter to make change for a customer. "Have a nice night," she said, in the flattest Texas accent I've ever heard. Then she turned back to continue her story, "An' his spare was flat."

Me and the guy behind me were both riveted. For anyone found in a Jiffy Mart at two A.M., it's the story of our lives — our spares are always flat. What's more, we all know what came next — after he got the spare fixed, the guy found out his jack was rusted.

The reason this fragment of a story struck me so plangent (I know it's a fancy word: Go look it up) is on account of it came the same week I met the queen of England, attended my college reunion, and covered the House redistricting debate. Not since the time I had to write about Elvis Presley's funeral in the middle of a Shriners convention and the World's Largest Cheerleading Camp have I had to cope with such an ungodly succotash of American culture.

Under the rules of covering the queen, as I understand them, the whole deal was pretty much off the record, so I can't report what delicious bon mots I laid upon the queen, nor what her scintillating replies were. She did say, twice, how veddy interesting (note that's not a direct quote). I'm told that two "veddys" instead of just "how interesting" is like hitting tilt on a pinball machine. It was like talking to one of those animatronic figures at Disneyland. This was at her reception for Texas journalists.

As Ken Herman of *The Houston Post* observed, "Sheesh, it's the same old crowd we always hang out with, except we're wearing better suits."

The whole queen thing, as G. Bush would say, left me in a state of high ambivalence. As one who suffers from an ingrained dislike of American Anglophiles (I suspect all of them would have been Tories during the Revolution), I was prepared to hoot raucously at the first sign of pomposity or pretentiousness.

On the other hand, here was this sweet-faced, grandmotherly woman handling one of the world's most awful jobs (how would you like having to meet hundreds of strangers almost every day?) with both dignity and grace. Leaves one with a combination of pity and respect. Her husband, as has been reported elsewhere, is a charmer.

The college reunion was more esoteric than

meeting the queen. I'm a graduate of Smith in Massachusetts, one of those heavyweight Eastern women's colleges. Our most famous graduates are Nancy Reagan, Julia Child, Betty Friedan, and Gloria Steinem, which is enough to give you some respect for the variety of white, middle-class women in this country. I'd not been back since graduation.

I read the statistical abstract on our class before I went, and groaned. Some appalling percentage of them did exactly what we were all expected to do: They got married within two years of graduation to men who went to Ivy League colleges, they all had 2.3 children, went into investment banking, have enormous incomes, and are living happily ever after, with vacation homes. I was sure I'd be a cuckoo in the nest — a left-wing, aging-Bohemian journalist, who never made a shrewd career move, never dressed for success, never got married, and isn't even lesbian, which at least would be interesting.

There are some verities of Eastern women's colleges that do not change — my classmates are *still* called Muffie, Midge, Chicken, Bitsy, and Tooters. But far from having sailed through life with both their fingernail polish and their self-confidence unchipped, they have collectively survived divorce, retarded children, cancer, alcoholism, discrimination, rape, bulimia, EST, hopeless marriages, aging parents, firings, gay children, nervous breakdowns — the class sounds like a whole season of Geraldo Rivera. Except they're still smart and funny and

45

gutsy, and a whole lot tougher and more compassionate than they used to be. Sisterhood lives. I left the reunion feeling oddly empowered, Smith having taught me once again what it was always supposed to — that women can do anything.

Meanwhile, back at the Lege, Harris of Pearland said to the redistricting chairman, "Please, Mr. Uher, please come to your senses before it's too late for the people of Brazoria County and all mankind." All mankind lost, 90–53. They wrestled in the hallways until past midnight; "But those are two of my best boxes!"

"Yeah, but those boxes are all Anglo."

"I'd rather have these Anglos than those Anglos."

Redistricting is the original form of nine-dimensional chess, the purest (only self-interest applies) and most complicated (it depends on party, race, class, supreme court rulings, demographic, economic, and sociological trends) form of political warfare. In brief, the Democrats won again, with some truly masterly district drawing, especially in Dallas County.

The effect of years of Supreme Court rulings is that the party in power can no longer cheat egregiously, especially when it comes to minority representation. But within the current limits of cheatability (known in the redistricting trade as "variance"), Texas Democrats have done themselves proud. The Republicans' only hope is that the Democrats may have outsmarted themselves. By trying to protect nearly every incumbent, they left thin margins across the board. A 53 percent Democratic district could easily be wiped out by, say, a Bush landslide in '92.

To Chairman Tom Uher and his committee, congratulations and a carton of Excedrin.

Dallas Times Herald, May 26, 1991

LEGISLATURE CONTINUES TO PLAY OSTRICH WITH SOCIAL PROBLEMS

The bizarre charm of our only Legislature was on entrancing display last week as about a third of the House of Representatives fled the capitol Tuesday night and took shelter in the governor's mansion, sort of like medieval dissidents escaping the power of the state by seeking sanctuary in a church. The Speaker locked the doors of the House so no one else could escape, police surrounded the mansion, and we were all pleased to see the tradition of festive antics we associate with Texas lawmaking still in fine and plummy form.

This particular mass bolt was an exodus of high principle, and worth examining in some detail, since it tells us a whole lot about the central pickle of governance today. One might even say the bolt was paradigmatic, had one not sworn off using the word *paradigm* (paradigms and a nickel'll get you a Coke).

The AWOL House members were on the losing end of a 69–6 vote to eliminate state funding for prekindergarten programs for three-year-olds. The prekindergarten program had received praise from national education experts and was considered the crown jewel of the Lege's recent efforts toward education reform.

It's essentially an extension of the Head Start–style programs that have proved so effective in boosting the academic performance and cutting the drop-out rates for poor and minority kids. So there we were, for once ahead of the pack in doing something really terrific for our kids who need it most, all hands basking in the praise, envy, and amazement of other states (not often you find Texas on the cutting edge in a deal like that).

And then comes this horrible budget crunch, huge deficits looming, Republicans as usual vowing to let kids rot rather than raise taxes, Democrats as usual too gutless to say anything except, "Me too, no new taxes."

So the kids get the ax and even that probably wouldn't have prompted a walkout, except, in one of those chilling conjunctions that occasionally make our problems too, too clear, the same day the House voted to save $206 million by cutting the funds for the prekindergarten programs, the House also voted to spend an additional $400 million to build new prisons.

It's a fairly well known fact that seven out of ten prison inmates are high school dropouts. As Representative Wilhelmina Delco of Austin said: "It boggles my mind. The very kids who would profit the most from education are also the ones who all indicators show will be the ones to go to prison."

Representative Curtis Soileau of Lumberton said: "What we are talking about is balancing the budget on the backs, the very small backs, of children. It is a price this state cannot afford."

Representative Glenn Maxey of Austin said, "When the vote came on the three-year-old kindergarten — the heart of education reform and one of the most meaningful programs for Hispanics and blacks and poor children — you had a situation where there was no leadership."

As I have pointed out time and again, it's a hell of a lot cheaper to send little kids to school than it is to let them grow up into young thugs who have to be sent to prison, not to mention the savings in the wear and tear on the nerves, property, and safety of the rest of the citizenry.

But the Republican arguments carried the day. Representative Troy Fraser of Big Spring, who proposed the cut, said: "How many of you are tough enough to cut a program that we have no idea whether it is working? We have to cut the budget. We have a $5 billion deficit."

Trouble with that argument is that we do know the Head Start programs work: There's more than twenty years of consistent tracking of better school performance and lower drop-out rates. But of course we have no money to spend on such programs because we keep having to spend all these ungodly buckets of dough building more and more prisons, none of which do a damn thing to lower the crime rate.

Stupidity, thy name is the Texas House of Representatives.

In general, this special session is one of those exercises in pain that induce sympathy for legislators even among the most cynical Lege-watchers. Boy, is it no fun to sit in the heart of Texas in the middle of the summer figuring out who to hurt next. And you know we don't pay these folks squat.

Double tuition for college students? Make it even harder for old folks to get into nursing homes? The interest of this session lies in the fair possibility that the state can save itself a substantial chunk of the impending deficit by juggling the bureaucracies around, more or less along the lines suggested by Comptroller John Sharp.

The efforts to reorganize the government more efficiently are welcome and long-overdue, but the deficit will still be sitting there devouring every hope of improving the quality of life in this state when they get through reorganizing.

The Lege is once more putting little patches on our leaky raft of state, stopping up holes and tears here and there with gum and spit, making little adjustments to our rickety, backward, regressive tax structure. The one thing they have failed to even consider is just sitting down and looking at taxes from scratch; looking at where the wealth is in this state and how to tax it fairly. And that is due to a failure of leadership on the part of Governor Ann Richards, House Speaker Lewis,

Comptroller Sharp, and all the major players in state government — with the exception of Lieutenant Governor Bob Bullock, who tried and got his head handed back to him on a platter.

Dallas Times Herald, July 28, 1991

HILL'S ALLEGATIONS HIT A NERVE WITH MANY KINDS OF WOMEN

Soap Opera City. Since only Judge Clarence Thomas and Professor Anita Hill know what happened between them, the rest of us are left trying to evaluate credibility and to figure out why this has become such a procedural mess. Seems to me one of the first points that needs to be addressed is the misplaced anger aimed at Hill by some senators and others, blaming her for the timing of her allegations against Thomas. Senator Strom Thurmond, in a stupefying display of hypocrisy, demanded to know, "Why didn't they come forward if they had something against him? Why did you wait until the day before the vote on him, the last minute, then bring in a woman saying it's ten years ago, ten years ago, she's charging him with sexual harassment. It just doesn't make sense." Turns out Thurmond himself has known about Hill's allegations for weeks: She's no last-minute surprise to him.

Another vein of complaint is why Hill didn't

file harassment charges against Thomas ten years ago. Talk about a question that answers itself. The woman's character, motivation, veracity, and common sense are being questioned in the most insulting terms. Senator Alan Simpson of Wyoming told the Senate that Hill "will be injured and destroyed and belittled and hounded and harassed" at the hearings. He later said this was not a threat, but that she would experience "real harassment" as a result of her allegations. As though sexual harassment weren't real. That, friends, is why women don't file sexual-harassment complaints. Precisely what is happening to Hill now is the reason women are reluctant to make public complaints.

One reason I find Hill credible is that there's nothing but unpleasantness in this for her. It is not a gratifying task. She cannot even be accused of being a publicity-seeker. She tried hard to keep her name and her charges quiet by following the prescribed procedures — it was the members of the Judiciary Committee who fouled things up by not investigating her charge, and they have no one to blame but themselves. And do we think there was some sexism in the committee's failure to follow up on her charges? Is George Bush a Republican?

Even I am surprised by the depth of the anger and resentment among women over the way Hill has been treated. I notice the anger is not limited to feminists or to professional women who would be the most likely to identify with Hill. Those in the pink-collar ghettos and even women who make their living by being beautiful are just as angry as longtime feminists. But a caution here, just because so many of us have endured sexual harassment (boy, didn't we all recognize the truck driver in *Thelma and Louise*) doesn't automatically make Judge Thomas guilty. We do have a right to be angry, however, that the male senators wouldn't take the matter seriously.

An ancillary problem here is the old one of whether private behavior is actually relevant to performance in office. As the right-wingers are so fond of pointing out, if one's private life is to be taken into public account, then Ted Kennedy, who is quite a good senator, would have been out on his ear years ago. A male friend of mine claims the "pig police" are becoming so zealous that before long none of us will be able to engage in friendly flirtation. That seems to me on par with the misplaced concern of people who worry more about the excesses of political correctitude than about racism and sexism. We have a long way to go before the imbalance is in that direction.

The Hill-Thomas debate can be passed by the same distinction that was useful during the confirmation hearings of the late Senator John Tower, who stood accused, y'all recall, of "womanizing." I go back to my earlier stand — I like men who like whiskey and women, nothing against them at all. But there is a difference between a man who comes on to a woman who is in a position to tell him to go soak his head, if she so chooses, and a man who hits on women who are economically or psychologically vulnerable. A boss who hits on his employees, a professor who hits on students, a doctor who hits on patients — that is abuse of power, it's not sex or flirting. And Anita Hill knew perfectly well that Clarence Thomas was in a position to damage or even ruin her career.

The palm for hypocrisy, at least so far, goes to Senator Orrin Hatch of Utah, who worked himself into a lather of indignation over the perfidious leaking of all this to the press. Hatch was so peeved at the idea that someone actually leaked private information to the press he could scarcely contain himself. Funny, isn't that the same Orrin Hatch who himself leaked to the press the contents of a very private and sensitive off-the-record conversation he had with Ted Kennedy not long ago?

Dallas Times Herald, October 12, 1991

SUDDENLY THE POLS UNDERSTAND THEY NEED TO DO SOMETHING

These are difficult days for those who are determined not to become cynics. Not since Manuel Noriega found Jesus has it been so imperative to keep in mind the difference between cynicism and skepticism. The voters of the nation — good on you all — have finally persuaded our elected leaders that we are seriously angry. The results are less appetizing than we might have hoped.

The sight of assorted geeks, dweebs, dorks, and bozos rushing in to propose middle-class tax cuts and national health-insurance plans is not for the weak of stomach. Our only president has finally noticed that he was elected to head the United States of America, not the New World Order. The Education President who spends more on military bands than on Head Start programs, the Environmental President who gave away one third of all our remaining wetlands, is about to get back to all that good old kinder, gentler stuff. Except, of course, for blaming the Congress for everything he hasn't done. Congress in turn is cordially blaming Bush for everything they haven't done. Oh, well, look at it this way — at least they know now we want them to do something.

It's an old poster — DO SOMETHING — but what's still startling in the aftermath of Tuesday's "wake-up call" is the extent to which our politicians still think they can get away with *appearing* to do something. Still government by public relations. Still presidential aides announcing that they need to work on the "perception" that Bush has no domestic agenda. They still haven't gotten it. The problem is not the perception — it's the reality.

Of the various middle-class tax-cut proposals, the one that makes the best sense is the one least likely to pass — Patrick Moynihan's proposal to cut the Social Security bite that comes directly out of our paychecks. As the debate finally begins about national health insurance, the skeptical-but-not-cynical citizen would be well advised to keep in mind that the American Medical Association has spent $10 million over the past few years in an advertising campaign to convince Americans that the Canadian health-care program doesn't work. The obvious rejoinder is — neither does ours. Nothing like firsthand information — try asking a few Canadians what they think.

At least we find amusement in the hard-core Republican opposition, this sudden burst of populist fervor. Representative Bill Archer of Houston, denouncing a House plan to balance a middle-class tax cut by putting a surtax on the richest people in the country, said, "It's an attempt to redistribute the wealth. It's not what we need to get out of the recession. It's bad economic policy." I am enchanted by this new grasp of redistribution of wealth. We are in the third term of an administration that has succeeded in radically redistributing wealth in this country from the poor to the rich. The fantastic concentration of wealth into fewer and fewer hands (the richest 1 percent of the people now have 40 percent of the country's total wealth) is the most striking fact of our recent history. We have a president who has vetoed the first increase in the minimum wage in thirteen years, vetoed any extension of unemployment benefits (paid for by a tax fund with a huge surplus into which we all contribute), and still wants to give a capital-gains tax break to the rich. Redistribution of wealth, what an appalling concept.

Dallas Times Herald, November 10, 1991

BEING AN "ARTHUR"

I had always envisioned the literary life or, as we used to say in East Texas, "being an arthur," as involving a lot of hanging out at Elaine's in New York City with terribly witty people. I have finally become an arthur and I find myself hanging out at obscure radio stations, trying to think of answers to questions like, "So, what *is* it about Texas?"

There are only two reasons to put yourself through it. The first is that your book is sure to sink without a trace unless you do TV and radio. (That tells you something about the power of print.) And the second is that writers who do it usually come back with at least one story to dine out on for the rest of their lives.

Myra MacPherson, author of *The Long Time Passing*, finally lost it upon arriving for some television show and finding the airhead hostess busy spraying her hair. "I'll bet you haven't even read the dust jacket," snarled MacPherson.

"What's a dust jacket?" inquired the airhead.

Liz Carpenter, author of *Getting Better All the Time*, once appeared on a chat show in Chicago with two dogs, one a Seeing Eye dog for a blind lady and the other a hearing dog for a deaf man. The dogs did not hit it off; they barked throughout the program and did their best to chew up all the guests and each other.

On another occasion, while touring for *Ruffles and Flourishes*, Carpenter arrived in Seattle with her hair so dirty she couldn't stand it. "My hair hadn't been washed for a week, it was solid spray," Carpenter recounted. "So when we got to the hotel, I started calling around to beauty parlors, but none of them were open at night. At last I found a lady who made house calls. She came to my room at eleven that night after a call-in show; I was willing to pay big bucks. As she was working on me, she said, 'You know, you're the first live body I've worked on for a long time.' She did corpses for funeral homes."

Jim Kunetka, author of *War Day*, arrived at a radio station to find the host in a tantrum, screaming: "That's it! I can't take any more! I quit!" And he stalked out two minutes before air time. Kunetka was thrown on the air with a producer frozen in terror who had not a clue about his book. So Kunetka spent an hour interviewing himself, beginning with, "Many people ask me . . ." As soon as he ran out of steam on one subject, he'd start again. "And I am also often asked . . ."

My pal Marlyn Schwartz is currently loping around the country, plugging her oeuvre, *A Southern Belle Primer: Or Why Princess Margaret Will Never Make Kappa Kappa Gamma*. She called avant-tour to inquire, "Have you decided how

61

you're going to sign your book?"

"Gee, haven't even thought about it. Probably something political, you know me — 'Keep fightin' for freedom,' or some such message."

"I'm signing mine 'Stay precious!' "

After Schwartz learned she was to be on the Phil Donahue show, she suddenly had new best friends. Her hairdresser called to say he would do her hair for free — just for a credit on *Donahue*. Ditto, the makeup artiste — wanted only a credit on the show. She went to the dermatologist to have a mole removed from her face. Upon learning she was to be on *Donahue*, the doctor cried, "Oh, let's take the ones on your neck off, too — they might pan in for a close-up."

"I can see the credit now," said Schwartz. "Moles by Mintner."

Ted Morgan, author of *On Becoming American*, once found himself on a Los Angeles show, sandwiched between Chubby Checker, the Twist king, and Nguyen Cao Ky, formerly the prime minister of South Vietnam. The host was so enchanted with Mr. Checker and his recollections of the glory days of Twist that, by the time he got around to Ted Morgan and his serious book on becoming an American, there was time for only a few questions. And by the time the host got to the former prime minister of South Vietnam, the time situation was dire. "Tell me, Mr. Ky," said the host. "Can you sum it up for us in thirty seconds — what went wrong?"

Dave Barry, the humorist, recently found himself in a greenroom with a sweet, appealing ten-year-old boy dying of AIDS. The boy and his mum went on just before Barry, both of them so courageous and winning that there wasn't a dry eye left in the house. Then the host said, "And now, Dave Barry to tell us about exploding cows."

Barry also wound up on a radio call-in show with Christopher Hitchens of *The Nation*, who is an authority on the "October Surprise" theory, the belief that in 1980 the Reagan campaign arranged to delay the release of the hostages in Iran to help defeat Jimmy Carter. First Hitchens would get a call about international skulduggery, then Barry would get one about boogers, making for a mad medley of snot and conspiracy.

Why publishers assume that one sells books through radio and television puzzles me. Wouldn't you think it would work better to place ads and interviews in print? After all, people who read newspapers and magazines are *readers*. But mine is not to reason why, mine is but to figure out an answer to, "So what *is* it about Texas?"

The extent to which the entire process is humiliating depends on one's sensitivity. I wanted to be a writer when I grew up, not a shill. On the other hand, a woman who loves Lubbock can't claim to have exquisitely dainty sensibilities. Being on a television show in between a segment on Cher's hairdresser and another on women who marry jerks is not the strangest thing that's ever happened to me. I was once banned from the campus of Texas A&M after students invited me to speak, because, the administration said, I might say something "political." (John Tower and Barry Goldwater had spoken previously — but that was different.) And, as I write this, a group of United States senators is on national television discussing breasts and penises. "Now, Professor Hill, when the judge was telling you how big his penis is, just how big . . ."

My fellow citizens, we live in a great nation. Its occasional resemblance to a lunatic asylum is purely coincidental and doubtlessly not the intention of the Author of Us All.

Mother Jones, January/February 1992

DEEP IN THE HEART . . .

My newspaper died the other day. I'd worked for the Dallas *Times Herald* for ten years, and its death was a kick in the gut the like of which I cannot recall ever having experienced. Worked for a lot of them; never had one shot out from under me before. Had no idea how much it would hurt.

"Like a death in the family," people kept saying. No. It was the death of a family. We were finally bought and then killed, just before Christmas, by our loathed rival, *The Dallas Morning News*, owned by the A. H. Belo Corporation. That's one way to beat the competition — buy 'em up and shut 'em down. It was done in a particularly brutal way, as Jim Henderson, our best writer, said that Sunday: "God damn Belo, wouldn't you know they'd do this on a day when the liquor stores are closed."

Setting aside the understandable sentiment of those of us who were attached to the *Times Herald*, what does it mean anymore when a newspaper dies? It may be a dying industry. It's sure as hell a sick one. Only some pitiful percentage of the population even reads a daily paper nowadays.

Perhaps Tip O'Neill's famous dictum, "All politics are local," applies to the newspaper bidness as well. There may be no Larger Lessons in the demise of the *Herald*, but I suspect, even allowing for my bias, that ain't so. I'm sorry if this sounds portentous or pretentious, but the death of the *Herald* is not just a sad, but a bad thing for Dallas. As all the world knows, Dallas, Texas, is a conservative, buttoned-up, uptight town, or at least that's its image. I worked there a long time, and I believe that Dallas, Texas, contains as great a variety of humanity as any place I've ever been — as many characters, eccentrics, drunks, reprobates, self-taught philosophers, and political apostates as, inch for inch, Manhattan, San Francisco, or Wamsutter, Wyoming (although Wamsutter does boast a sign in its only café that says PICKLED EGGS AND NO ARM WRESTLING). One of my ambitions is to retire to Wamsutter eventually and start a newspaper called the "Wamsutter Bumfucker."

But the weight of conformity tends to fall heavily in Dallas — the conformity of dress and behavior and thought. It's not hard to be different in Dallas. It's just harder. When I first started writing there, about gun control and abortion, among other things, folks would come up to me and say, "Oh, I do so admire your courage for saying that." What courage? I just stood up and said what I thought — b.f.d. The death threats died down after a while. Longer I worked there, more I realized there were huge numbers of folks in Dallas who didn't like or agree with the town's prevailing ethos; but they so seldom heard from anyone else who thought the same way they did, they figured it would be wise to keep their mouths shut.

Those were the people who needed the Dallas *Times Herald*. Sure, it was only a half-assed liberal newspaper — but that was still more ass than any other paper around had. Deep in the heart of Texas, we supported gun control, a woman's right to choose abortion, social-service spending, and Ann Richards for governor. Across town was a newspaper that was still running editorials in the mid-seventies using "nigger dialect" to ridicule welfare recipients. A paper whose record on race, Vietnam, ecology, and social welfare was not only deplorable, but ugly as well.

In the early eighties, Virginia Ellis and Dale Rice of the *Herald* embarked on a chilling series about the conditions in nursing homes for old folks in Texas. I remember it in terms of smells. Most nursing homes smell of urine because old people become incontinent and that's part of the human condition, not because of poor care. But old people who are left to lie in their own filth for days at a time, old people who have huge, festering bedsores, old people who get no medical care for weeks — those old people produce a different smell. If you've ever smelled it, you never forget it. The *Herald* stories were the equivalent of a big strong whiff of that smell.

The *Herald*'s editorial page under Jon Senderling followed the Ellis-Rice series with one salvo after another. We clung like a burr to the issue — from the first tentative steps toward reform in the Texas legislature, to the committee hearings, and then through the final bills and debates. Many of our colleagues in the press corps accused the *Times Herald* of crusading. Yes, crusading! They said we'd lost our objectivity on the "nursing-home issue." But vultures who leave old people to lie in filth for days at a time in order to increase their own profits are not one side of "the issue" or "the other side of the story." They're slime bags. We did not give them equal space in our newspaper. So hang us.

We often held up a mirror to the city of Dallas, and sometimes Dallas did not like what it saw. So it blamed the mirror. We not only proved with enormous amounts of computer time and effort that the entire system of criminal justice in Dallas is hopelessly flawed by racism, we actually worked to free those wrongfully convicted (in a city that values law 'n' order more than the Bill of Rights). Lenell Geter, who was doing time for robbing fried-chicken joints; Randall Dale Adams, who was supposed to have killed a Dallas cop; Tony Woten; and others all know that it makes a difference if there are two newspapers in town.

T'warn't all guts and glory at the *Herald*. We loved a "good murder" and could be as shallow as the next paper on many occasions. We also made some truly wiggy endorsements from time to time. But the *Herald* had an endearing antic streak, as well: It introduced Joe Bob Briggs along with the concept of drive-in movie reviews to the world. Any newspaper that can make you laugh out loud almost every day deserves some credit.

Oddly enough, the *Herald* kept making money. But it was bought sequentially by two entrepreneurs who were leveraged up to their eyeballs, and every penny that the paper made went to pay off the interests on those debts. When you put no money back into a newspaper, it is a death sentence. We might still have made it in a healthy economy, but there it is, just another casualty of the eighties.

I first sensed the *Herald*'s coming doom on New Year's Eve 1985, when Ernie Stromberger, who had been the paper's entire Austin bureau back in the sixties, was drunk as a boiled owl at Sam Kinch's annual New Year's bash. We had been chewing over the latest changes at the ever-troubled *Herald* when Ern rocked back on his heels in the Kinch garage, plastic glass in hand, and announced, "Management . . . was never the strong point . . . of the *Herald.*"

"Damn, Ern," says I, somewhat spiflicated myself, "that's plangent. We ought to carve it into the marble on the front of 1101 Pacific Avenue." I know an epitaph when I hear one.

Mother Jones, April/May 1992

LOOKING FOR WORK

"Looking for work is now your full-time job," intoned the announcer in a spiffy little movie now showing at the Texas Employment Commission. I missed *Hook*, *The Addams Family*, *The Prince of Tides*, *Cape Fear*, *Bugsy*, *JFK*, and *Father of the Bride* over the holidays, but I'm prepared to critique *How to Apply for Unemployment Compensation* with any interested cineaste.

It may not be zippy, but I believe *How to Apply* compares favorably in its genre with the immortal short *The Left Turn* seen so often in defensive-driving courses.

Harold, the guy sitting next to me during one showing of *How to Apply*, was filling out his forms during the film, which you're not supposed to do — you're supposed to give full attention to the cinematic masterwork — but I wouldn't rat on a fellow unemployment statistic. Under "Kind of work wanted," Harold put down "cas worker." Then he wrote, "parol officer." It may be a long winter for Harold.

Down at the unemployment office, we're fairly buddy-buddy. One of the rules is, "Do *not* bring children," but many mothers do, because who has the money for a baby-sitter, and little kids crawling all over is a pretty good icebreaker during the long waits. Unemployed people spend a lot of time waiting. Still, there is the understanding that every one of us who finds a job leaves one less job out there for the rest of us.

I keep having to mark "Other" on my forms under "Reason for leaving." Did not quit, was not fired — wouldn't you think they'd have a category in the form by now for "Employer went belly-up"?

While sitting in the Texas Employment Commission office, I enjoyed reading about George Bush's discovery that we're in a recession. He found this out when he got a new chief of staff — a fellow named Skinner — in the White House. Skinner also informed the president that a recession means a lot of people are out of work, so the president promptly expressed his sympathy for us.

All of us waiting at the TEC appreciated that. Then came the headline that said, GM TO CUT 74,000 JOBS. I like reading about the economy, which I find is a livelier entity than I had previously given it credit for. The economy sometimes takes "a sharp dive, from which it will arrange a quick ascent." Said ascent not having come to pass, the economy is then observed "consolidating its position for the improvement."

John Kenneth Galbraith has detected a new wrinkle in the "chamber-pot theory" of the economy. This is where the recession causes a steep downslide, followed by a very flat bottom and then an equally steep recovery. The economy has athletic skills: "The economy is now wrestling with the final stages of recession." The economy gets around: "The economy is now contending with a temporary roadblock in its path to recovery."

This is, of course, all horsepoop. As Galbraith pointed out in a speech to the National Press Club, "The present recession is not an autonomous, self-correcting economic drama. It is a wholly predictable response to the speculative extravagances and insanities — and the specific government policies — of the 1980s.

"We are paying," Galbraith said, "for the mergers-and-acquisitions mania which left around a third of our large corporations with a heavy, sometimes crucifying burden of debt. And we are experiencing the consequences of an extreme and often mindless speculation in urban real estate. And of the junk-bond miasma. And of legislative and regulative measures that, in effect, put government funds — guaranteed bank and S&L deposits — at the disposal of some of the fiscally most extravagant and felonious entrepreneurs since John Law and the South Sea Bubble."

Don't cry for me, Texarkana. I still have one job. I'm a columnist for a national magazine based in Madison, Wisconsin. Will write for food.

The Progressive, February 1992

72

GIBBER AND OTHER MISDEMEANORS

God, we're going to miss House Speaker Gib Lewis. It's not often we get a target like that in public office (come to think of it, it's not all that rare either — look at our last governor, and the one before that, and the one before that, and the one before that). The Gibber has been providing peerless entertainment at the capitol for ten years now, and his retirement announcement January 8 devastated fans of Texas legislative oddity. Despite the trying legal circumstances surrounding his retirement (those pesky misdemeanor indictments to which he is so prone) the Gibber left with his head held high and a song in his heart.

In his farewell address to the press (the watchdog of democracy) the Speaker spake thusly: "You've cost me a lot of money, a lot of time, a lot of embarrassment, and probably a political career." Singling out his hometown newspaper, El Gibber added, "Why should I do anything for the *Fort Worth Star-Telegram*, which has repeatedly over the years absolutely destroyed my ass? I mean, you all, Number One, got my ass indicted on a goddamn speculative deal. You have never shown me any goddamn consideration at all. Why should I show that goddamn newspaper any consideration at all? I mean, just think about it. I don't need you son-of-a-bitches and apparently you all don't need me up there. I hate to be that blunt about it."

The Gibber gave us so many moments to remember. Both his tongue and his syntax regularly got so tangled that his language was dubbed Gibberish and provided the state with wonderful divertissement. He once closed a session by thanking the members for having extinguished theirselfs. Upon being reelected at the beginning of another session, he told members he was both grateful and "filled with humidity."

When anxious to press forward with legislations, he would urge members to "disperse with the objections." He once announced, "This is unparalyzed in the state's history." Other Gibberisms: "This legislation has far-reaching ramifistations." "It could have bad ramifistations in the hilterlands." "This problem is a two-headed sword: It could grow like a mushing room." "We don't want to skim the cream off the crop here." "We'll run it up the flagpole and see if anyone salutes that booger."

In Gibberish, anything unusual was "adnormal." If he was confused, "There's a lot of uncertainty that's not clear in my mind." Economic diversity kept coming out as "economic versatility." And the budget could be cut through "employee nutrition."*

This may be apocryphal, but Lewis supposedly once replied to a teacher who criticized his syntax, "What sin tax? I'm not for any sin tax. I'm against all new taxes."

Then there was his immortal performance on Disability Day, 1985: Disability Day is when the state of Texas honors its handicapped citizens for their efforts to get better access to public buildings. We never appropriate a nickel for the purpose, but we always honor their efforts. So both houses just resoluted up a storm, the governor issued a proclamation, and the Gibber presided over the joint session. Public access for the handicapped at the capitol is not all that great, but a bunch of them managed to wedge their wheelchairs into the back of the gallery. The Speak read both resolutions and the proclamation and didn't make hardly any mistakes — we were all so proud. Then he looked up at the gallery and said, "And now, would y'all stand and be recognized?"

But Texas politicians who have difficulty expressing themselves are seldom, in my experience, fools. Perhaps the most poignant moment I ever had with Lewis was the time he called me into his office late one sine die night and asked if I

*Gib Lewis's last great contribution to the political lexicon came after a special session in November 1992, called to resolve Texas's school-financing crisis. The session ended in total failure. Lewis said, "I think they're just beatin' their heads against a dead horse."

would please stop making fun of the way he talks. "My mother," he said gently, "was an English teacher." I damn near cried. It's not nice to make a proud man look like a clown — but I could never resist his more creative manglings of the language. On the other hand, I never mistook him for a fool either.

Those who know Lewis only through the headlines describing his indictments and questionable dealings must by now assume the man is a hopeless sleazebag. Actually, he's a helluva hard guy to dislike. If you met him, you'd enjoy hangin' out with him: He's kind and he's fun. I have always suspected he is a fundamentally decent, well-intentioned person. But I do not know how to account for his repeated violations of ethical conduct, whether they were illegal or not. I used to describe him as "ethically challenged" and once, in a fit of exasperation, observed that he has the ethical sensitivity of a walnut. He just didn't get it.

The trip to Ruidoso in 1984 on the racing lobbyists' tab. The trip to Pebble Beach on the taxpayers' tab. The trip to South Africa as a guest of the South African government. The time in 1986 he had to reimburse his political campaign fund for $25,000 he had "mistakenly" used to purchase stock for his company's retirement program. "Just one of those dumb things," said Gib, with one of his Alfred E. Neuman grins. The time he failed to report his business interests held jointly with lobbyists because he "ran out of room on the paper." The time he had Parks and Wildlife stock

76

his ranches with fish and game and then defended himself by saying, "I have been he'pin' Parks and Wildlife for seventeen years: If they owe anybody a favor, they owe me a favor." This is a prime example of the Extenuatin'-Circumstance School of Texas Political Ethics. Since I doubt Gib Lewis ever intended to be corrupt, he was honestly indignant and hurt when people accused him of it — shame-on-those-who-think-evil was his usual reaction.

But by the end, there just weren't any more excuses. He was actually indicted in 1991 for the same damn thing he had to plead "no contest" on back in 1983 — failure to report. In '83 it was failure to disclose business interests he held jointly with lobbyists — in '91 it was failure to report a gift of money from lobbyists. Even the D-U-M-B defense wouldn't work. I don't know why he did it. Anyone with his record who couldn't see that letting lobbyists pay for an eight-hundred-dollar-a-night hotel room in Mexico was going to look terrible, whether it was illegal or not, has, well, the ethical sensitivity of a walnut.

In his own way, in his own context, in his own time, Gib Lewis was a good Speaker. Which is to say, by the values of a time mercifully past, he was a fine "members' Speaker." He was largely nonpartisan, fair to Republicans, fair to just about everybody. He tried to make sure the members didn't have to vote on issues that would cost them politically — the stuff they really hate, like abortion. He did not invent, but he certainly carried to a fine art the tactic of dodging controversial and costly issues until whatever the problem was had festered so long the courts had to intervene and declare whatever-it-was unconstitutional. This clever ploy enabled all the pols to blame the damned old interfering federal judges for whatever costly remedies they were then forced to undertake.

The tactic is sinfully irresponsible, but it sure makes life a lot easier for pols, and that's who kept reelecting Lewis Speaker.

The best I ever saw Gib Lewis do was in the wake of sine die night of the sixty-ninth session, 1985. The indigent health-care bill died in the waning moments of the session, killed by Republican Representative Bill Ceverha of Dallas, a notorious meanie. Mark White called a special session for the next morning. The senate passed the bill in thirty minutes. The House, with the governor's aides all over the floor, referred the bill to the Health Committee chaired by another Republican right-winger, Brad Wright. Gib Lewis came into the committee room and stood directly behind Wright, like a rather menacing cigar-store Indian, as the committee took up one conservative amendment after another. The message was clear — no Democrat was to vote for any of them at the expense of the Speaker's personal displeasure.

The Republicans then introduced a noxious substitute bill on the floor and the good bill's sponsor, Jesse Oliver, moved to table. The motion passed 73–71, but the Republicans called for verification and got a 71–71 tie. Gib Lewis always wielded a mean gavel — he has broken them innumerable times — but I never heard him hit a lick as hard as he did that afternoon. The vote was stuck at 71–71, the vote was held open, arms were being twisted clean out of their sockets, but it was still tied. The Speaker, by custom and common sense, almost never votes — it's bad form. Suddenly Lewis said, "The chair votes Aye" and whacked the gavel down so hard it sounded like the crack of doom. And that's why poor people no longer die on the streets outside clinics and hospitals in this state.

But aside from a very few such shining hours, Lewis's unprecedented ten-year tenure as Speaker was marked not so much by his ethical bloopers as by a dated Texas concept of what government is for — to create a healthy bidness climate. It was Lewis's habit, motivated by his desire to prevent "his" members from having to vote on anything tough, to work out accommodations in which all the affected parties were represented. And by all, I mean every lobbyist with a stake in the outcome. It was the era of the "done deal," lobbyists for corporate special interests sitting down with the elected representatives of the people on an equal footing to hammer things out. In fact, the lobbyists often appeared to have more clout than the legislators, so that the only party not represented in the back room was the public. That's why we so often got government of the monied special interests, by the monied special interests, and for the monied special interests. And Gib Lewis honestly never saw anything wrong with that process. He thought he was doing the right thing.

He was wrong.

The Texas Observer, February 14, 1992

GONE WITH THE WIND

On the very same day the president of the United States puked on the prime minister of Japan, we lost House Speaker Gib Lewis here in Texas. You may have missed the latter event in the excitement over the former, but in the Great State the headlines were all about the Gibber's retirement after ten years. A few days later Gibber pleaded *nolo* to two misdemeanor counts — his traditional plea when faced with indictment.

Back in the days when Jim Wright of Fort Worth was Speaker of the U.S. House of Representatives and El Gibber was Speaker of the Texas House, they were known as "the stereo speakers."

It was a close-run thing, getting the Gibber to announce he wouldn't run again. Last October 1, a state judge threw the Speaker in jail for failing to show up at a hearing, and Lewis said, "You know what my thought was on that day? Stay here and kick somebody's butt." Happily for the judge, the Speaker reconsidered and decided to retire to his gummed-label empire in Fort Worth.

The bad news is this means a Speaker's race, perhaps the nastiest single form of politics, after redistricting, known to man. The Speaker is elected not by the people but by the 150 members of the Texas House of Representatives, with heavy input from the Lobby.

At this point, the leading contender is Dicknose Laney from Lubbock. His real name is Pete, but the resemblance of his proboscis to a penis caused him to be politically christened Dicknose years ago.

Dicknose is OK by me, because his entertainment potential is real high. He has an odd habit of frequently telling the truth. Last year, faced with one of those classic special-interest battles where one set of wretched rich folks square off against another set of wretched rich folks, Laney was asked which side he was on. "Whorin' just as fast as I can," muttered Laney. "Whorin' just as fast as I can."

Meantime, our only president, after displaying his diplomatic finesse in Japan, went out on the campaign trail to show off his political skill.

"Don't cry for me, Argentina," he told the people of New Hampshire. "Message: I care."

In his George-Bush-Man-of-the-People mode, he carefully changed "starting" to "fixin' to start," and then quoted lyrics from a country band he identified as "the Nitty Gritty Ditty Great Bird."

Some have interpreted his stump performance as evidence that he needs to stop taking Halcion because he's wigging out, but as a veteran Bush-watcher I can assure all hands that what we have here is merely George in his excess-of-exuberance mode. That's the one that frequently causes people to conclude that the man's a dork, whereas he sees himself as simply being spirited and amiable.

Of more concern to a suffering citizenry is the news that the White House still thinks Bush's drop in popularity is attributable to "failure to communicate." In other words, they think it's a public-relations problem. Since Ronald Reagan solved every political problem with public relations, Bush thinks he can do likewise.

But since PR doesn't actually solve problems, Bush is now stuck with all the little horrors that have been quietly mushrooming during eleven years of neglect while America's attention was diverted by winnable little wars and other cunning diversions.

In the meantime, the Democrats are marching militantly in the wrong direction. As the economy stalls out, the Soviets are in dire need of aid, and this country is in almost equally dire need of investment in both people and infrastructure, the *vogue du jour* is for a middle-class tax cut. What a bright idea: Let's increase the deficit.

It does raise the always timely question: Is God punishing us?

The Progressive, March 1992

GOOD MORNING, FORT WORTH! GLAD TO BE HERE

Hidy, Fort Worth. Think of the fun we're going to have. The statehouse, the courthouse, the White House — mirth, glee, and hilarity to be found in abundance everywhere we look. It requires, of course, a strong stomach to laugh at politics in our time. But the only other options are crying or throwing up, and they're bad for you.

It is not my habit to write columns about writing columns, a subject about which damn few people give a rat's heinie. But since I'm new to y'all and y'all are new readers to me, I thought I'd start by telling you where I come from and a little about how I look at all this — then you can take my diamonds of wisdom with a grain of salt or a pound of salt, depending on your preferences.

I believe politics is the finest form of entertainment in the state of Texas: better than the zoo, better than the circus, rougher than football, and even more aesthetically satisfying than baseball. Becoming a fan of this arcane art form will yield a body endless joy — besides, they make you pay for it whether you pay attention or not.

It's all very well to dismiss the dismal sight of our Legislature in action by saying, "I'm just not interested in politics," but the qualifications of the people who prescribe your eyeglasses, how deep you will be buried, what books your kids read in school, whether your beautician knows how to give a perm, the size of the cells in Stripe City, and a thousand and one other matters that touch your lives daily are decided by the dweebs, dorks, geeks, crooks, and bozos we've put into public office. (You may believe yourself in no peril of ever landing in Stripe City, but should you happen to contravene a law made by the only politicians we've got, this too will become a matter of some moment to you. For example, if you happen to possess six or more phallic sex toys, you are a felon under Texas law. In their boundless wisdom, our solons decided that five or fewer of the devices make you a mere hobbyist.)

While it is true that I believe all politicians are in a free-fire zone, and further that it is an important American tradition to make fun of people holding high office, I also believe there are heroes in American politics. They're just in damn short supply. I also believe Texas legislators are overworked and underpaid. But that doesn't excuse their performance.

Ronnie Reagan, who was not the brightest porch light on the block, used to go around proclaiming, "Government is not the solution; government is the problem." Me, I think government is a tool, like a hammer. You can use a hammer to build with or you can use a hammer to destroy with. Whether government is good or bad depends on what you use it for and how well you use it. On the whole, it's a poor idea to put people in charge of government who don't believe in using it.

I believe government should be used in order to form a more perfect Union, to establish justice, ensure domestic tranquility, provide for the common defense, promote the general welfare, and secure the blessings of liberty to ourselves and our posterity. God, as the architects say, is in the details.

I believe that all men and women are created equal. That they are endowed by their Creator with certain unalienable rights. That among these are life, liberty, and the pursuit of happiness. I believe that governments are instituted among men and women, deriving their just powers from the consent of the governed, to secure these rights. And that whenever any form of government becomes destructive of these ends, it is the right of the people to alter or abolish it.

I dearly love the state of Texas, but I consider that a harmless perversion on my part, and discuss it only with consenting adults. If Texas were a sane place, it wouldn't be nearly as much fun. Twenty-five years of reporting on Texas and I still can't account for that slightly lunatic quality of exaggeration, of being a little larger than life, in a pie-eyed way, that afflicts the entire state. I just know it's there and I'd be lying if I tried to pretend it isn't.

I am so tickled to have Fort Worth as a home base. I've loved the town for years — it seems to me characteristic of Fort Worth that it still thinks of itself as a town, not a city. Dallas is a city. My great-aunt Eula lives in Fort Worth. Once when I was visiting, I said to Aunt Eula, who's had that same black telephone for at least forty years, "Aunt Eula, have you ever considered getting a new phone? You know they make them now in a lot of different colors and fancy shapes."

Aunt Eula said, "Why would I want a new one? This one is perfectly good." I think "Perfectly Good" should be Fort Worth's municipal motto. Another time, when I was driving for Aunt Eula, she said, "Turn left where the green water tower used to be." I am contemplating writing a guide book to Fort Worth with "Turn Left Where the Green Water Tower Used to Be" as the title, it being the kind of town where everyone knows where the green water tower used to be.

When Jan Morris, the famous British travel writer, wrote a piece on Fort Worth several years back for the *Texas Monthly*, she of course flat fell in love with the place, as all right-thinking people do. For years I've feared that Fort Worth would be "discovered" and become chic and self-conscious. Horrors. I raced over after Morris's gushing article came out to see if any damage had been done. It was the talk of Juanita's, and I joined several prominent citizens, many of whom had been interviewed by Morris, in mid-discussion.

They all thought the article was "real fine, real nice."

"So interesting about Jan Morris," I said. "You know she used to be a man." One of the fundamental Fort Worth expressions, benign puzzlement, settled on every face. "Yep, she used to be John Morris and she was a don at Oxford and a famous mountain climber, but then she had this sex-change operation and now she's a woman, but she still lives with her ex-wife, 'cause they love each other." Silence ensued. Finally one of them said, "Well, she seems like real nice folks." The others all nodded and said, "Yep, real nice folks."

Fort Worth is a town where people know what's important.

Fort Worth Star-Telegram, March 1, 1992

ELECTION CROSS FIRE REOPENING WOUNDS OF VIETNAM YEARS

Anyone who was over seventeen in the late sixties and early seventies will recall one of the constant social refrains of that era: "Oh *God,* let's not spoil the party by talking about *Vietnam.*"

But someone always did, remember? And all those wedding receptions and family reunions and Saturday-night beer busts would wind up in the same awful acrimony. If it was an intergeneration gathering, the dads and uncles who had served in WW II were wont to foghorn forth with great certitude about the lily-livered longhairs who hadn't the courage to serve their country.

Theirs was the Good War. Ours sucked, and one of the many tragedies of Vietnam was the generational divide it created.

During George Bush's State of the Union address this year, he paid tribute to the gutsy qualities of young Americans who had served in the military from WW II, when they wrote "Kilroy was here" all over everything, to Desert Storm, when they wrote "Elvis lives." So moving, that brash, sardonic irreverence in the face of war. Bush skipped a war, of course. In Vietnam they wrote "F.T.A." all over everything (young readers will please consult their elders for the full translation).

Some of us thought Vietnam was finally over on November 13, 1982, when the Vietnam veterans built their own memorial and gave themselves their only homecoming parade.

Others thought Vietnam was resolved at last by Desert Storm, when that blizzard of yellow ribbons blanketed the country as though to say, "No matter how dubious the enterprise, this time at least we will not make the mistake of blaming those who got stuck fighting this thing."

But now, as though it were 1969 again, there is a great collective groan, "Oh, *God,* let's not spoil the election by talking about *Vietnam.*" But there it is.

Governor Bill Clinton of Arkansas, still the front-runner among Democrats, got out of serving in Nam — first by taking a student deferment, then by considering ROTC, and finally by registering for the draft lottery at a time he had zilch chance of getting drafted. If that makes him a draft dodger, so are those in the great majority of that generation of 26 million American men who were eligible to serve in the military during those years.

It's not easy to bring back the context of those times, but a rather good way to start is to read the letter Bill Clinton wrote his draft board in its entirety. Not the snippets you see quoted here and there for journalistic oomph or the carefully chosen quotes used for nasty political sniping, but the whole.

It was the time when there were no good choices. Clinton does not make a perfect case: Many who felt and believed just as he did wound up making different decisions. One said, "I agreed with everything Clinton wrote, but with me there was one more thing. I had a kid brother a year younger. I kept thinking, suppose I take the out I've got and then they draft Tommy and he gets killed over there. Then how will I feel?"

Those who now feel entitled to blame the young men who once had to choose among all those bad choices are playing an old, evil game — blame the victims.

It wasn't the Bill Clintons, who hated the war, or even the Dan Quayles, who supported it but got out of fighting, who got us into the misbegotten folly that was the Vietnam War. Nor was it the young men who made Vietnam the most class-ridden war this country has ever fought.

The Selective Service System was deliberately set up to protect the elite and to use those who had started life with fewer advantages than their cohorts.

The war in Vietnam was fought disproportionately by poor, less educated kids, disproportionately by black, brown, rural, and Indian kids. General Lewis Hershey, then head of the Selective Service, laid it all out for you in a disgusting little pamphlet entitled *Channeling*, which set out the SS's MO.

Those bright enough and rich enough to get into college were exempt. Those headed for certain elite professions were exempt. Those doing socially useful work, such as teachers, were exempt. But Lord help the average Joe on the fast track to nowhere. Those who were "not college material" were cannon fodder. God, it was cold.

Myra MacPherson, author of *Long Time Passing*, a wrenching look at Vietnam veterans, described one of the most disgraceful legacies of Vietnam, Project 100,000, which eventually took in more than 350,000 "volunteers."

The project took men with marginal minds and bodies who had been previously rejected from the draft and promised them remedial education and an escape from poverty. And then it sent them to Vietnam.

Recruiters concentrated on urban barrios and ghettos and Southern rural back roads. They took young men with IQs as low as 62. In 1969, the year Clinton got out of the draft, the project rounded up 120 men from the Oakland ghetto; 90 percent of them scored less than 31 on the military's application test. Ridiculed by their fellow soldiers as the Moron Corps, they, too, died disproportionately in Vietnam.

What matters most for the purposes of this election and of this country now is not who went and who got sent to Nam or who stayed home and why, but the commitment of each of the candidates to the proposition that no American should be asked to die or to kill for an unworthy purpose. And that if war comes, its cost should be paid equally by all.

The odd flip side of the draft-dodger debate is the way it is being used by the candidates themselves to prove they are sufficiently bloodthirsty to let it all happen again. Bill Clinton says it's OK that he skipped Nam because, by God, he supported Desert Storm. Bob Kerrey says he can't be attacked for opposing the war on Iraq because he was a hero in Nam. The implication is that only if you are a veteran or a warmonger are you fit to be president.

This is not a hypothetical issue. Last week, *New York Times* columnist William Safire, whose Republican credentials include a stint as Richard Nixon's speech writer, spelled out the "comeback scenario" for George Bush. His three-part plan for Bush's political resurrection includes a tax cut and stealing the Democrats' thunder by scheduling meetings with big-deal foreign leaders around the Democratic Convention.

Then Safire went on to what he called "the Spring Surprise." Safire notes that the White House has been setting up a case against Saddam Hussein of Iraq, Kim Il Sung of North Korea, and Muammar el-Qaddafi of Libya.

"Does it strain credulity to suggest that at least one of these three dictators is going to get zapped?" inquired Safire. "I think not. . . . If Bush's stern warnings to three dictators about threatening the peace turn out to be empty posturing, then, and only then, would President Bush reveal himself to be too weak to deserve re-election."

Start a little war to prove how tough you are? Now, there's a swell idea. I just wish, twenty years after Vietnam, I believed that the sons of the George Bushes and the Bill Safires who have these crackerjack notions would be the ones to die for them.

Fort Worth Star-Telegram, March 3, 1992

DON'T BELIEVE ALL YOU READ — LIKE BUSH'S LIPS

Some days you open the newspaper and it's sort of like finding Castro in the refrigerator. What to our wondering eyes should appear last week but the intelligence that George Herbert Walker Bush of Kennebunkport, Maine, had reared back on his hind legs and announced, "Life means nothing without fidelity to principles."

Have to take a deep breath after reading that one, don't you?

Let's see — abortion, no new taxes, civil rights, Vietnam, voodoo economics, catastrophic health insurance, the Clean Air Act, a kinder gentler nation, being the Environmental President, being the Education President, ransoming hostages, and so much more I can't even remember half of it.

Wouldn't you think the Weathervane President would be better off quoting Emerson about how consistency is the hobgoblin of little minds?

I don't think it's fair to call Bush to account for his most nonsensical promises. He pledged to wipe out illiteracy, and concerning drugs, he vowed during his inaugural, "This scourge will stop." Since no one believed him at the time, who cares?

But he has been a consistent crusader for one issue, never swerving, never giving up. He wants a capital-gains tax cut. When he asked for it again in his State of the Union address this year, the Congress actually laughed, which I thought was a trifle tacky of them. To give you an idea of just how wrongheaded that proposal is, consider the stunning new bottom line on the eighties. We all know the eighties ended with the rich having gotten richer and the poor poorer, while the middle class shrank.

But now comes word that it's worse than we thought: No less than 60 percent of the wealth created during the eighties went to the richest 1 percent of the people in this country. Sixty percent of the wealth to 1 percent of the people. And the effect of a capital-gains tax cut, of course, is to make the rich even richer.

The Congressional Budget Office study that produced the stunning 60 percent figure actually contains even worse news. An additional 14 percent of the new wealth went to those families in the top 2 percent; another 20 percent went to those in the top 20 percent, leaving a grand sum total of 6 percent of the new wealth to be distributed among 80 percent of the people. The average family saw its income edge up 4 percent to $36,000, while the bottom 40 percent of families saw their income decline.

The New York Times quoted Paul Krugman, MIT economist, who said: "We know that productivity has increased since 1977 and that more people are working. Where did all that extra income go? The answer is that all of it went to the very top. The number that no one had seen was how much of the growth went to a few people."

There really is such a thing as obscene wealth. The other day they were going to nick Michael Milken for another $500 million to pay for the lawsuits over his financial machinations, on top of the $400 million he's already paid; but the FDIC wouldn't take the new deal because they think Milken has too much left. Now $900 million happens to be the exact amount this country needs to pay for its share of United Nations peacekeeping operations in 1992 and 1993. But it looks as though the Congress won't cough up the money for the U.N. because the federal budget is already strapped.

The U.N. is keeping peace in Cambodia, Yugoslavia, El Salvador, and Western Sahara. That's a lot of lives that could be saved by one man's fines — without even leaving him broke.

Fort Worth Star-Telegram, March 8, 1992

EXERCISE THE RIGHT TO VOTE OR GIVE UP THE RIGHT TO GRIPE

The Citizen Who Does Not Vote Loses His Right to Complain. So it's not in the Constitution. It's one of the unwritten rules of being American, like, Nobody Can Sing the National Anthem.

Besides, voting freshens your breath, improves your sex life, and prevents unsightly hair loss. So get out there and do it, and let's hear no more malingering from you whiners and slackers about how there's nobody you want to vote for. It's a glorious year for you None-of-the-Abovers, with protest candidates of the highest quality.

If you're a Republican and you're fed up, you can vote for Pat Buchanan. If you're a Democrat and sick of the whole system, Jerry Brown's the man for you.

My fearless forecast is that Brown will do better than expected in Texas. I base this not only on the enthusiasm of the students at the University of Texas at I-35, but also on the existence of an organization called Matrons for Moonbeam.

98

Question: What would happen to Brown's face if he smiled? Second question: What would it take to make him smile?

Yankees keep asking me, What is the mood of Texas voters? How are Texas voters feeling? I think Texas voters have PMS. Moody, cranky, and snappish. What else could it be but a mass case of PMS? Avoid caffeine and stress, troops, we'll feel better in the morning.

The scummiest ad of the political season so far: in the South Texas state Senate race between Eddie Lucio and Juan Hinojosa, a Lucio ad in which a photograph of Hinojosa is doctored to make him look like the devil, with pointed eyebrows and a sneering mouth. Chuy Hinojosa, by the way, is one of the most decent people who ever served in the Texas Legislature. But no point in getting into even low dudgeon about South Texas politics.

One of my favorite ads this year came from a much-harassed South Texas county commissioner (two opponents!). He decided to cut to the chase and took out a full-page ad that said, "ACTIONS SPEAK LOUDER THAN WORDS." Then he spent the rest of the page listing the streets that will be paved during his next term. I like this straightforward approach; in fact, it reminds me a lot of what George Bush has been doing lately.

Democrats are having a hard time finding reasons to vote against Bill Clinton. Calling him "Slick Willie" hardly seems fair, despite his tendency to be facile. Paul Tsongas is always there being fatally unfacile. Tsongas grows on you, but only slowly.

Clinton does not seem to have been hurt by the Gennifer Flowers brouhaha or by the phony allegations of draft dodging or by this new flap over having a real estate investment with an S&L maven. All of which caused Dave Barry of Miami to observe in jest, "I don't think sticking up that grocery store is going to hurt him either, nor that thing with Madonna, nor . . ."

Sign of our changing times: At Bill Clinton's wind-up grand finale here, a South Texas *pachanga* on Sunday night, the food was free, but they wouldn't let anyone eat until after the candidates had spoken, and the beer, my dears, was $1.50. So much for tradition.

The Democrats keep telling us there is no such thing as a free lunch, while President Bush races around the country tossing goodies to the populace. Keeping up with political trends in this great nation requires a great deal of flexibility.

Meantime, hail and farewell to Iowa Senator Tom Harkin, who dropped out of the presidential race yesterday. Harkin billed himself as the only "real Democrat" in the race, but it turned out to be a bum year for those proudly billing themselves as part of the old politics.

Harkin never managed to explain that he meant *really* old politics, as in Franklin D. Roosevelt's politics. Since there are relatively few voters still with us who can remember FDR's politics, the message went nowhere.

There are even fewer who know what populism actually was. The word is currently used by the political press corps either as a synonym for racist demagoguery (as in "David Duke is a right-wing populist") or as a synonym for "pissing on rich folks for political profit."

The real populists, who for a moment in history came close to Thomas Jefferson's ideal republic, created a movement that transcended both race and class around the proposition that there should be some democratic influence on our financial institutions.

Despite Harkin's poor showing, it's still a good idea.

Fort Worth Star-Telegram, March 10, 1992

A GOOD FIGHT OR TWO
KEEPS POLITICAL SHOW
MOVING RIGHT ALONG

What a tasty array of political flaps we have to munch on.

Rubbergate is bouncing along nicely. The edifying sight of our elected representatives dancing about like so many cats on a hot tin roof is perking up many a jaded citizen.

The Newt Gingrich–Tom Foley duke-out was swell entertainment, while the Jerry Brown–Bill Clinton verbal fisticuffs, a brisk bout on Sunday night, had fight fans out of their chairs.

Biff. Bam. Pow. Great stuff.

Students of scandal are taking lots of notes on Rubbergate. I like the reaction of California congresswoman Barbara Boxer, who has contributed fifteen dollars for every check she bounced to the U.S. Deficit Reduction Fund. The ones who whine that it was all the bank's fault for not letting them know get no points. Cooler heads keep pointing out that this is not an actual scandal, on account of no misuse of public funds is involved. It is, they argue, an embarrassment instead.

Don't you hate people who stop in the middle of a perfectly good argument to insist that everyone define his terms?

The only trouble with the increasing peppy Democratic nomination fight is that we have now reached the point where taking the most popular position seems necessary and inevitable. Alas for Paul Tsongas, who started out doggedly telling people some truths they didn't really want to hear. He's still at it, but he's being drowned out by Jerry Brown, who it turns out is now racing around Michigan with a UAW jacket on over his turtleneck, denouncing the free-trade pact with Mexico.

In a state full of laid-off and about-to-be-laid-off auto workers, that sells well. I hate to see politicians get votes by playing on people's fears, but Jerry Brown is at least half right.

The free-trade pact with Mexico will encourage the corporate greedheads to move their plants south of the border so they can exploit poor Mexican workers. The free-traders are also right. Long term, it's a good economic deal for both us and Mexico. This is a deal where God is truly going to be in the details. The only way American workers will come out ahead on this is if our government includes some serious money for worker retraining, serious environmental safeguards, and a whole lot of other stuff I, for one, don't think the Republicans have any intention of including. At least, the Bush administration has shown no signs of doing so thus far.

So American workers will get shafted unless this deal is done very carefully indeed — the way you'd uproot and replant prickly pear.

The other Great Protectionist in the race is Pat Buchanan. I must confess, I find it difficult to follow Republican ideological squabbles. Reminds me of the declining days of Students for a Democratic Society, when all these humorless, passionate people would stay up all night arguing furiously over some utterly obscure point of doctrine having nothing to do with real life.

The man keeps whining that George Bush is leading us away from the glory days under Ronald Reagan. *What* glory days?

Was I living in some other country than Pat Buchanan? All I saw was an incredible concentration of wealth at the very top of the society, the tripling of the national debt, an orgy of leverage buyouts and mergers and acquisitions that crippled the economy, the S&L rip-off we now have to pay for, increasing callousness toward the poor and homeless, a president who ignored the AIDS crisis and everything else about health care, crime and pollution increased, and the average citizen got nowhere.

On the other hand, we did beat Grenada in a fair fight.

So now Buchanan wants to get us back to those good old days by:

A. Shutting down the National Endowment for the Arts, and

B. Paying people to buy American cars.

What politicians mean when they blather about "competitiveness" is that Americans should make cars so good you don't have to pay people to buy them.

For some reason, President Bush has been terrified by Buchanan's odd campaign (Bubba and all the guys down at Booger's Lounge spend just an awful lot of time worrying about the National Endowment for the Arts).

Since Bush already broke his read-my-lips word on taxes once, Buchanan's got him terrified of doing it again, so now he's stoutly vowing to veto the economic package coming out of Congress because it increases taxes on people who make over $200,000 a year. I suppose Buchanan *would* attack Bush for "raising taxes" if he signed the package. But who else does Bush think would be upset?

The people who make over $200,000 a year, of course. But isn't that the point of this whole political year — that what is becoming increasingly clear is that we are all tired of having this country run primarily for the benefit of people who make more than $200,000 a year?

Fort Worth Star-Telegram, March 17, 1992

LET'S QUIT CHEWING ON RUBBERGATE AND TACKLE REAL ISSUES

Rubbergate gets funnier and funnier. The sight of Secretary of Defense Dick Cheney, surrounded by generals dripping with brass, explaining it all to us with charts and pointers was too fabulous.

Didn't you expect General Schwarzkopf to show up any minute to explain, "First the check went here, then we made an end run around the bank balance, but the enemy recorded the maneuver on its high-tech satellite, so . . ."

Now, the president says that for all he knows, *he* might have bounced some checks when he was in the House — 'cause the whole system was so screwed up.

This reminds one of the theme song of the John Wesley Hardin Fan Club (not to be confused with the John Dillinger Died for You Society): "He wasn't really bad / he was just a victim of his times."

The excuse for misbehavior and even crime, which liberals are prone to ponder but which con-

106

servatives have always rejected with righteous indignation, is that one's environment has something to do with how one behaves.

Hey, if a sixteen-year-old kid whose mama was on drugs and whose daddy decamped before he was born, who grew up in the projects surrounded by drugs and crime, who gets abused by his stepfather and sent to a crummy school where he never learns to read; if that kid winds up committing a crime and it's all his fault, how come Newt Gingrich was writing bad checks? Did Tom Foley really make him do it?

Wuss of the Year Award goes to the Minnesota congressman who made his wife stand up and take the blame. He stood there with his arms crossed, like, "Boy, is she gonna get it when we get home."

The ineffable Charlie Wilson of Lufkin, who disappointed many of his fans by appearing so low on the list of the Big 24, observed, "Piety must be a terrible burden to try to bear through one of these things."

And unctuous self-righteousness even worse.

Don't you think some group of Capitol Merry Pranksters ought to at least short-sheet Gingrich's bed? Your Responsible Observers — David Broder springs to mind — are concerned lest all this lead to some dire loss of faith in government, a debilitating degree of cynicism that might even damage democracy.

Nah, let the sun shine on them all: We've got enough sense to take a real close look at he who casts the first stone.

Bill Clinton, who has not yet been accused of writing bad checks, has been trying out an interesting line of late: "Look, I'm not a perfect person." As a qualification for the presidency, it has a certain charm.

We are now living in an oddly confessional culture — television chat shows from Oprah to Geraldo to Sally Jessy to Jenny Jones are peopled by citizens "sharing" with the rest of us what it is like to be married to impotent partners, or a victim of incest, or to be a cross-dressing dwarf. It is enough to make one yearn for a resurgence of that fine old New England trait, reticence.

The trouble with this chat-show confessional genre is that rather than increasing genuine empathy for those suffering life's more outrageous slings and arrows, it remains a shallow, titillating form of entertainment, designed more to appeal to our prurient interests than to extend our understanding. It may be true that we are all sinners, as Jim Bakker and Jimmy Swaggart were so fond of reminding us, but the sad fact is that many of us still prefer to dwell on that comforting, self-righteous sense that sinners and even victims are Very Different from ourselves. *They* deserved it.

What would happen if we all grew up enough to admit that we aren't perfect and neither is anyone else, even granting that some of us come a lot closer than others? I'm not qualified to address what the effect on our immortal souls might be, but it sure would go a long way toward curing the hypocrisy and self-righteousness that mar our politics.

Then, when we hit a Rubbergate, instead of having to watch these disgusting displays of either abasement or blame-shifting, we would find pols with the sense to say: "There it is. It's wrong, so let's change it."

And then we could all get back to worrying about more important stuff, like how to fix the economy, make some progress toward social justice, and get rid of the designated-hitter rule.

Fort Worth Star-Telegram, March 19, 1992

JUST MIGHT NEED A POLITICIAN FOR THIS GOVERNMENT THING

Since we are currently at a pass when no one in her right mind would stand up and defend politicians in front of God and everyone, let me say a few words in behalf of the breed.

One of the oddest facets of this election year is that we have all become experts on electability. All over the country Democrats have solemnly made their pronouncements: "I like Paul Tsongas, but I don't think he's electable." . . . "Jerry Brown is saying a lot of good things, but I don't think he's electable." . . . "I'm not crazy about Clinton, but I think he's electable."

Great, a whole nation of political mavens. But the knock on Clinton is that *he* may not be electable precisely because he is what we're all mad at this year — a politician. A shade too glib, a touch too facile, christened "Slick Willie" by the biggest newspaper in his home state. (That the biggest newspaper in his home state happens to be an archconservative, Republican paper should be taken into account. It's as though everything you knew about Ann Richards you got from *The Dallas Morning News*.)

There is an extent to which I like politicians who are good at politics. And Bill Clinton is. To put together the kind of organizations that won him Texas and almost every other state he's run in is no easy feat.

It speaks well for his ability to control and direct huge, unwieldy entities — and that is what government is.

Nixon, another effective, though despicable, politician also managed to get the enormous sloppy contraption that governs us to crank around and actually produce something. As Tom Wicker points out in his book on Nixon, the man had a far more successful domestic presidency than he is credited for.

Henry Cisneros recently observed that governing has become the art of sighting that tiny sliver of daylight in the wall of obstruction thrown up against change and squeezing through it to get something done. I submit to you that the ability to do that calls for the skills of, well, a politician.

My own weakness for bomb throwers is reflected in my fondness for candidates like Jerry Brown, who would just as soon raze the whole system to the ground. But failing a revolution, wouldn't it be pleasant to have someone in office who knew how to get the government to work? George Bush, who was advertised as "ready on Day One," may or may not know how to get government to work, but since he doesn't seem to want it to do anything, apart from giving rich folks a capital-gains tax cut, the point is moot.

Bush, the man with no ideas, is now about to run a campaign blaming the Congress for preventing him from doing the nothing he has in mind, but it won't wash. Eisenhower worked successfully with a Democratic Congress (controlled by Sam Rayburn and Lyndon Johnson, both pols to the bone.) Nixon worked successfully with a Democratic Congress (controlled by Tip O'Neill, also a politician to the bone.)

In addition, Clinton has that Happy Warrior mentality that marks the good politician: He *likes* doing this. He likes meeting and greeting and schmoozing and baby-kissing and back-slapping: He likes people. You'd be amazed at how many politicians don't. One recalls the early years in office of Lloyd Bentsen, who was wont to wade into crowds offering his hand like a dead fish and looking as though he wished the peasants had washed better before they came to meet him.

As to what ends Clinton would use the great machine of government, should he get hold of it, none of us knows. He initially positioned himself as a DLC Democrat — that's the Democratic Leadership Council, Chuck Robb and the like, folks who call themselves neoliberals, Atari-Democrats, and such. I always thought of them as Republican wannabes. They said they would marry Democratic compassion with Republican efficiency, both suspect currencies at this point.

Clinton has some claims to populism. In fact, the people who put his Texas campaign together were mostly bomb throwers themselves twenty years ago, and they still think he's with them: Maybe they're right.

The most interesting thing about this election is the widespread understanding of how high the stakes are. The end of the current recession, which they keep promising us has just hove into view, is not the end of our economic problems. People understand that the economy is on a long-term slide, recession or no.

Another boom like the one we had in the eighties will just leave us weaker. We need an industrial policy, an energy policy, an investment tax credit, and a whole variety of measures to make capital more productive and business more competitive. We can't beat the Japanese with Adam Smith.

The other gnawing source of our discontents is the realization that the entire social fabric is shredding. The country is not only not better off than it was four years ago, or twelve years ago, it is also a less civilized place to live.

Crime, poverty, schools, the environment, homelessness, drugs, health care — none of it is better. The feeling that the country is unraveling is pervasive. George Bush's response is to pretend the only thing wrong is the presence of "Carping Little Liberal Democrats."

This inspired a Democrat in Houston to found the CLLD's, whose motto is "More carp, less crap."

Fort Worth Star-Telegram, March 21, 1992

STIRRING PROSPECTS AHEAD

O what a year it was — already. Only March and we've already had Gennifer with a G, we've had Paul Tsongas doing his tortoise imitation to victory, we've had the Jerry Brown boomlet and the Bob Kerrey surge. We've had Pat Buchanan — whose heroes are Francisco Franco, Joe McCarthy, and Cardinal Spellman — standing up for Americanism.

And now the whole road show has come South, with the usual disastrous consequences. Because of the cherished national myth that all Southerners are borderline morons, there is a noticeable dumbing-down of political rhetoric, which was already at bumper-sticker level.

I've been cogitating ways to counteract this insidious stereotype, to get us up to speed, image-wise. I'm contemplating opening a restaurant called Bubba's Trattoria, which will serve tiny medallions of chicken-fried steak on top of cream gravy, with patterns in the gravy made with chicken gizzards; tiny medallions of spareribs on top of barbecue sauce, with patterns in the sauce, and a coleslaw made with radicchio and yellow and red peppers. We'll offer Campari long-necks and Lone Star spritzers. Think it'll do any good?

Maybe not. Another progressive magazine called the other day to ask if they could change a reference in my column from George Dickel to Jim Beam, so the yuppies would understand it. Fellow Southerners, are we sure we *want* to get up to speed?

But the man who deserves our most respectful attention this month is our only president, George Bush. Every time Bush steps out to campaign, one is left wondering, "Why dudn't he just go puke on some other Japanese official?" Or, "Maybe he should go buy some more socks at J. C. Penney's." As a federal drug-enforcement official observed, "They've got the President to stop taking Halcion. That was the year's bright spot for the war on drugs." Many a plaintive searcher after truth has called here in recent weeks seeking enlightenment — what is wrong with George? Is it the Halcion? Is he scared of Buchanan? Does he have a plan? Why isn't he sticking to his plan? Why did he fire John Frohnmayer, the arts guy?

The prevailing assumption is that George is off his feed. That there's disarray in the White House. They haven't got their act together. Their act is falling apart. But no, fellow citizens, I am here to assure you that this is Normalcy City for George Bush. He's not losing it. He was always like this. So he goes to New Hampshire and says, "Don't cry for me, Argentina. Message: I care." He sounded like that when he ran against Lloyd

116

Bentsen for one of Texas's Senate seats in 1970. I promise. His preppy dweeb tendencies are standard, not asymptomatic.

Of course, he may be feeling more culturally deracinated than usual lately on account of his home on the range — well, actually, his pied-à-terre in a Houston hotel — just went into bankruptcy. Yep, Chapter 11 for the Houstonian Hotel. As a lady at Harvard Medical School once said to an applicant who had killed his parents, "Well, these things do happen."

But lest you think that, because of this fast early start, the fun is about to die down and the whole presidential race will become serious, sober, and respectable, fear not! There are intimations of wonderful things to come. Bush is already desperate enough to have brought up his dead baby again to prove that he too knows what suffering is, recalling the wonderful dead baby-off of 1988.

Bill Clinton is attacking Tsongas for being insufficiently enthusiastic about the death penalty (Tsongas wants it reserved for those who commit major crimes against society, like big-time drug dealers). This development promises that we will see on a national scale the same fry-off that so enlivened the 1990 Texas governor's race, in which each of our candidates vowed to fry more felons than the next.

Stirring prospects ahead, fellow citizens.

David Duke and Pat Buchanan are womping away on illegal immigration, racial quotas, blas-

phemous art, and deadbeats on welfare — all those things that account for our faltering economy.
    Nothin' but good times ahead.

The Progressive, April 1992

LEGAL ANSWERS WON'T RESOLVE ABORTION FIGHT

Far away from the screaming demonstrators and screaming counterdemonstrators so hopelessly divided over a woman's right to choose to have an abortion, away from the television cameras and the posturing, away from the pushing and shoving and the harassed cops, in the solemn, quiet hush of the Supreme Court, the only action that really counts on abortion took place last week.

Those who witnessed it said the atmosphere was curiously deflated, they felt none of the tension and suppressed excitement that normally accompanies major arguments before the Court. The Pennsylvania case, *Planned Parenthood* v. *Casey*, turns on five restrictions on women who choose to have abortions — one of them patently silly, one potentially devastating for a few minors, and the others apparently reasonable, or at least, as the law puts it, "not unduly burdensome" on the surface.

On reading the transcript of that argument I felt — and Sarah Weddington, the Texas lawyer who argued *Roe* v. *Wade* in 1972 and who was in the court last week, confirms — that perhaps the critical moments occurred when two judges asked essentially the same question. Justice Sandra Day O'Connor asked the woman lawyer for the American Civil Liberties Union and Justice Harry Blackmun asked the male attorney general of Pennsylvania, in Blackmun's words: "Have you read *Roe*?"

It is a bit like trying to bail out the ocean with a teaspoon to make this point again and again in the face of so many people who are convinced otherwise, but *Roe* v. *Wade* did not give women the right to abortion on demand. *Roe* sets up a trimester framework, in which the state's interest in protecting fetal life increases as the fetus becomes viable (able to live outside the womb). Only the mother's life or health takes precedence over the fetal life in the third trimester.

The two most troubling restrictions in the Pennsylvania law are the requirements that a married woman inform her husband and that minor women get the consent of their parents before they can have abortions. You could sort of see the justices goggling at the first requirement: O'Connor wanted to know if there were First Amendment implications in compelling speech. She also asked about the First Amendment implications of compelling doctors, as the Pennsylvania law does, to describe a great long list of fetal development, options, and social services.

The best information available indicates that 95

percent of married women seeking abortions do inform their husbands, as the vast majority of teenagers also inform at least one parent — if they have one they can find. The problem is with the exceptions and the sometimes tragic consequences of state-ordered communication. A woman legislator in Pennsylvania, when the notify-your-husband provision was being debated, proposed a law that would require husbands to notify their wives before having an affair. Her point, of course, was the absurdity of the law requiring communication in a family where communication has broken down.

The Pennsylvania law is silly in that it vitiates its own requirements: The exceptions to the husband-notification requirement are medical emergency, when the husband is not the father of the child ("I'm going to have an abortion, dear, but don't worry, it's not your child"), when the husband cannot be found, when the pregnancy is the result of a reported sexual assault, or when the woman believes it is likely she will be physically abused. Somehow all this, according to the Pennsylvania attorney general, will "further the integrity of marriages." O' Connor was clearly intrigued by the odd discrimination involved — unmarried women in Pennsylvania are not required to notify the fathers.

If you have ever talked with minor girls who apply for the court's consent to get an abortion rather than notify their parents, you understand something of the wretched tangle of violence, incest, and physical abuse that afflicts so many families. When legislatures go about putting restrictions on abortion as though every family consisted of Ozzie and Harriet and two darling children, they add another terrible burden to lives that are already almost unbearable. You cannot save the life of an unborn child by driving its mother to suicide.

A particularly thoughtful letter-to-the-editor last week noted that those on both sides of this issue who harass others and break the law "do not have a commitment to the movement beyond meanness and revenge against uppity women and/or super-righteous Christians." The feminists' claim that many who profess to care for "unborn children" are actually more interested in controlling the behavior of women is sometimes evidenced in the most comical ways. *The Wall Street Journal* carried an account of the Battle of Buffalo last week that included a vignette of a sixty-nine-year-old man shouting at a pro-choice woman: "You *have* a choice: Stop screwing around." Oh, dear. Well, there are still a few people who think that's what's at stake.

But far from the madding crowd, where the majesty of the law comes into play, the issues, oddly, seem more nakedly clear. The only question is: Who is to decide? The government or the individual? A government that has the power to make a woman bear a child she does not want also has the power to make her abort a child she does want. The two apparent polar opposites here — actually flip sides of the same coin — are China and Romania. In China, the government forces women to have abortions; in Romania, until recently, the government forced women to have one child after another after another, with awful results. In both countries, there was state control over women's wombs.

I would love to be able to "split the difference" on this terrible question, to be able to say, in gooey Pollyanna fashion, "Let's all work together to prevent unwanted pregnancies." Settling the legal questions on this issue will not settle the moral ones, but I cannot believe it is wise to give government the power to make these decisions.

Fort Worth Star-Telegram, April 26, 1992

THE BILLIONAIRE BOY SCOUT

Piece of work. H. Ross Perot. He's the best right-wing populist billionaire we've got in Texas, so if you don't like him, you're out of luck.

Everyone wants to know, "Is he serious?" In politics, that means, "Does he have any money?" Friends, Ross Perot is as serious as a stroke.

By and large, Perot has been a good and valuable public citizen in Texas. He is invaluable when he knows what he's talking about. No one has plumbed the depths of his ignorance, but one subject he does know is education, from what's wrong with teacher training to the most arcane reaches of how to finance public schools. Ross Perot has been an unalloyed force for the good. Over the years, he has given enormous sums through his foundation to educational experiments and improvements, though no one knows how much because one of the most attractive things about him is that his philanthropy is usually anonymous.

His good works range from sending in a SWAT team of tree experts to try to save Austin's beloved old Treaty Oak after some nut poisoned it (tree died anyway) to quietly helping the families of

MIA's and other veterans.

But he has also mounted some damn peculiar crusades. In the late seventies, he headed up a War on Drugs — and like everyone else who has ever done so, he lost. This was in the days when first-offense possession of any amount of marijuana was a two-to-life felony in Texas — wasn't as though you could have gotten tougher on drugs. Perhaps his most famous crusade was "Tell It to Hanoi!," an effort to succor and free the American POW's held by the North Vietnamese in the early 1970s. While Perot focused the nation's attention on the plight of sixteen hundred American prisoners in North Vietnam, Richard Nixon continued to prosecute the disastrous war in the South, killing millions. "The North Vietnamese cannot understand how we Americans value the lives of even a few men," said Perot.

Perot brought his "Tell It to Hanoi!" campaign to the Texas state capitol in 1971 on what may still be the single weirdest day in the history of that peculiar institution. Jets roared over Austin in "missing-man" formation, while beneath the rotunda, in hour after hour of bloodstained oratory, brows were darkened and teeth gnashed over the fate of Our Boys. It was a patriotic orgy, although, as the *Texas Observer* noted at the time, no one uttered a peep about exactly what Our Boys were doing over there when they got caught. One received the impression that they had been mysteriously kidnapped while distributing gum to small children; almost all of them were professional military pilots engaged in the heaviest aerial bombardment in history.

"Is there any question what our grandfathers and great-grandfathers would have done for sixteen hundred men held prisoner only a day's ride from Austin?" cried Perot, who then explained that Hanoi was only twenty-four hours away by air, and we should saddle up, ride out, and get 'em. He further urged the state of Texas to deploy a delegation of local leaders to confront the Pathet Lao and the Viet Cong and to demand the release of Texas POW's. Our then-governor, known to all as POP Smith, for Poor Ol' Preston, was intellectually challenged by the task of getting from the mansion to the capitol every day. You could almost hear the entire Legislature gulp at the mind-boggling prospect of POP Smith debating the Viet Cong.

Ross Perot is fundamentally a superb salesman. So superb that it amounts to a form of genius. Over the years, he has become far more sophisticated in his analysis of political issues, but he retains the glib salesman's tendency to reduce complex realities to catchy slogans. In the old days, he advocated, as a cure for poverty, teaching the Boy Scout Oath — to do my best, to do my duty, to God and to my country — to every child in the ghetto. Let's face it, it's not sufficient.

He is still given to the sort of sweeping statements he made twenty years ago: "Pollution? That's an easy one. No question about it . . . Give me the choice of having all those industries dumping pollutants into the rivers or the choice of having no factories, and I'll have the factories. I can clean up the rivers in five years."

This is not a man who has grasped the concept of dead oceans. American Perot-nistas bear a superficial resemblance to the Argentine variety. What we have here is a strongman, a right-wing populist: no party, no program — just a cult of personality. All he needs now is an Evita.

Once when Juan Perón was returning (he was always returning), the *Peronistas* stopped cheering after he had passed by and commenced shooting one another, having nothing in common other than their allegiance to Perón. One suspects the Perot-nistas (the coinage is by novelist Peter Tauber) will have the same problem, though one trusts not as dramatically.

It's hard to envision a seriously short guy who sounds like a Chihuahua as a charismatic threat to democracy, but it is delicious to watch the thrills of horror running through the Establishment at the mere thought.

There is always a superficial attraction to the notion of an outsider coming in to clean up a corrupt, wasteful political system. "Let's send Ross Perot up there," cries Bubba. "He knows how to kick ass." Successful "bidnessmen" have been running for office in Texas for years on that appeal: "Vote for me; I've met a payroll; I understand the bottom line." We have been plagued in recent years by rich guys bored with making boodle who decide to take up public service instead. An entirely commendable impulse, but why don't they start by running for the school board or the county commissioners' court? Why do they always want to buy the governorship or a senatorship? Or, in the case of Perot, who's richer than God, the presidency? It's enough to make you yearn for the good old days, when rich guys just bought racehorses and yachts.

Because when these rich guys get into office, we find they're disastrous as political leaders. They're so accustomed to working in hierarchical, top-down organizations — where they can fire anyone who doesn't jump high enough — they go berserk with frustration when nobody jumps at all. You can get elected governor, but you can't fire the Legislature, or even the Egg Marketing Advisory Board. Our last Big Rich Governor was Bill Clements, '87 to '91, who, when he tried to learn Spanish, inspired the observation, "Good, now he'll be bi-ignorant."

It's a rotten year to try to defend generic politicians, but the critical political skills — negotiation, persuasion, compromise, coalition building, patience, and the willingness to listen to fools more or less gladly — are still minimal requirements in public office. The ability to kick ass, one finds on sad assessment, is not often useful.

Bush may know how to get the machinery of government to work, but since he clearly has no ideas about what he wants it to do, the point is moot. Look, we're all desperate for an alternative this year. Perot is appallingly straight — he truly

is out of Norman Rockwell by the Boy Scouts —
but that doesn't mean he'd make a good president.
Nor is he without flaw. For one thing, he's the
world's first Welfare Billionaire; he made his gelt
by using computer software developed by the government, and then he charged the feds handsomely
for their own invention. The closed-door congressional investigation into those charges will finally
get some much belated but long-needed attention.
All that and more will come out if and when he
runs.

In the meantime, you Perot-nistas can console
yourselves with what I believe is a heretofore utterly unreported fact: H. Ross is a genuinely funny
sumbitch. I often teased him in my old *Dallas
Times Herald* column, reporting outlandish assertions about his activities. ("H. Ross Perot announced yesterday he had purchased the Lord God
Almighty, the ancient though still serviceable
deity, believed by many to be the Creator of the
Universe.") I once announced to an astonished
world that Perot is a communist, worse, an agent
of the Kremlin, on account of he had attacked the
entire foundation of the Texan way of life — football. Right in front of God and everybody, Ross
Perot said the trouble with Texas schools is too
much football.

Imagine.

He got into the habit of calling me after these
japes to make semi-droll response: "Yew said in
yore column my mind is only a half an inch wide.
Well, all my friends say yore wrong. They say

it's only quarter of an inch." Followed by that Chihuahua bark of laughter, "Har-har-har."

Then one day I put into print a glaring error about Perot. I was holding forth on one of the more devastating imbecilities of the Reagan era, the abolition of the progressive income tax in favor of a two-tier flat-tax rate. I ended this screed by observing, "And so you see, if you make more than $17,500 a year, you will now be in exactly the same tax bracket as H. Ross Perot." And then, because my high school English teacher taught me to write balanced sentences, I added, comma, "who makes more than $1 million a year." I knew Perot was Big Rich and figured it was a safe assertion, but I did not check. Next day the guys on our bidness desk in Dallas called, laughing their asses off. "Ivins," they said (you think I'm making this up, but they spoke in tandem), "H. Ross Perot makes a million dollars a *day*."

Well, kiss my chicken-fried steak. I didn't know Kuwait made a million dollars a day. I'm settin' there thinkin', "Damn. This is gonna be an embarrassing correction." Then the phone rings, and an operator says, nasally, "H. Ross Perot calling collect for Molly Ivins. Will you accept the charges?"

I didn't even have the presence of mind to tell the cheap sumbitch to call back on his own nickel. Perot came on and poor-mouthed, still soundin' like a Chihuahua — got fired from his job at GM, couldn't get his own company back, and here's me usin' him as an example of some big rich guy;

didn't I even read my own newspaper, et cetera. It was the funniest gotcha anyone ever pulled on me.

But just 'cause this guy is my favorite Texas billionaire doesn't make him fit to be president. "Gummint" in my home state has almost always been run by folks who think the purpose of gummint is to create a healthy bidness climate. The result is that Texas is Mississippi with good roads. I wouldn't wish that on the rest of the nation.

It says right at the top of the Constitution what government is supposed to do: "Form a more perfect Union, establish justice, insure domestic tranquility, provide for the common defense, promote the general welfare, and secure the blessings of liberty to ourselves and our posterity." It doesn't say anything about the bottom line. Nothing wrong with running government in a bidnesslike fashion — that's why you should appoint some penurious s.o.b. as Secretary of the Treasury. But we need more from our government than bottom-line thinking. As that goofy guy from Baja Kennebunkport said, we need some of this vision thing.

Time, June 1992

READ MY LIPSTICK

Trying to save populism from the fangless inanity to which the American political press keeps trying to consign it is damn near full-time work these days.

The next reporter who refers to David Duke as a populist ought to be Bushururued, as they now say in Japan, meaning to have someone puke in your lap. The press declared Jimmy Carter a populist in 1976 because he carried his own clothes bag. Hell, the man wasn't even a peanut farmer, he was a peanut processor, but try to find anyone who cares about that distinction. The president of the United States was recently deemed to be strutting his populist stuff by stopping in for a splash of beer at a South Texas honky-tonk during a dove-hunting trip. And even Ronald Reagan, God save us, was styled a populist because he had antiestablishment support.

So few political writers know anything about populism — it's like trying to explain a sunset at a convention for the congenitally blind. Calling David Duke a populist is like calling Pat Buchanan a global visionary: message — Zulus are coming.

It tells us far more about the elitism (now there's a good populist word) of the media-ocracy than it does about populism.

The easy and ignorant equation of populism with racist demagoguery is largely the intellectual legacy of Richard Hofstadter, the U.S. historian we all had to read in college. In *The Paranoid Style in American Politics* and other works, Hofstadter relegated the populist movement, perhaps the only truly democratic movement in our history, to the Father Coughlin Memorial Ash Can. The irony, of course, is that real populism was an interracial movement, so powerful that it transcended not only race, but class and the vicious sectionalism of the day as well.

Racism was used by southern Democrats to help destroy populism — it was not part of populism. True, both Tom Watson and Cyclone Davis, among the great populist leaders, became vicious racists, but that was only after they had forsaken populism and returned to the "party of the fathers," that is, the Democrats.

The other current meaning of populism is "pissing on rich folks for political profit." This can be done with varying degrees of suaveness: Denouncing "malefactors of great wealth" gets you more points than noting that bankers all have hearts like caraway seeds. Nevertheless, the genteel political press is united in its judgment that bashing rich folks is unseemly. Worse, it is passé. Barney Frank, that exemplar of liberalism, said recently, "Americans just don't accept a class analysis." True, but they do know when they've been screwed.

Perhaps the press should not be blamed for its sad perversion of populism. As Lawrence Goodwyn, the great historian of the populist movement, has observed, we no longer have the political vocabulary to describe the notion of a substantial democratic influence over the nation's financial system. We don't even know how to talk to one another in a truly democratic way anymore, much less do we retain the sense of autonomy and possibility about politics that would give us hope that there is something *we* can do to fix things.

The problem is far older than the cold war, during which anyone who criticized capitalism could be stigmatized as a com-symp. Goodwyn traces the demise of the democratic dream back to 1896, the year that marked the death of populism's formal political structures. Thomas Jefferson's idea of elementary republics, units of about a hundred people making decisions together, was, toward the close of the last century, actually realized in Populist Alliance halls throughout the South and the West. We have never come close to it again.

Ironically, the need for what we lost when populism died keeps asserting itself more and more strongly. If the times do indeed create the leaders, a new Sockless Jerry Simpson is due to appear among us at any moment. (Sockless Jerry was elected to Congress as a populist from Kansas in 1890 and defeated in 1894. He was one of the finest orators ever elected, and probably the worst speller as well.)

Our amorphous, New Ageish yearning for self-esteem — and fumbling for ways to find it, teach it, and learn it — is a direct though apolitical reflection of the essence of populism. As Goodwyn writes in *The Populist Moment*, "At bottom, Populism was, quite simply, an expression of self-respect."

The cooperative movement of the 1880s and 1890s gave U.S. farmers — black and white, tenants and landowners — collective self-confidence at a time when they were being so ruthlessly exploited by the banks and the railroads that it can still make your teeth hurt to read about it. Populism also developed and spread political education and leadership in a unique fashion. Each suballiance had its lecturer; each county had its county alliance and county lecturer — hundreds of local leaders listening to, learning from, and then expressing the needs of people, and all of them fashioning remedies. It was not a programmatic movement; it had no ideology. Its prescriptions were pragmatic, considering only what needed to be done and what worked. And let us not forget, the populists supported women's suffrage.

Having lost that sense of the possibility of change through cooperation, we have retreated to individualism and materialism; we are now so passive about politics that at best we only watch it on TV. We have been reduced to the politics of bumper stickers.

135

The crying need of our time, of course, is for ways to democratize capital. The populist movement, with its from-the-ground-up structure, developed a variety of forms to do precisely that, many of which may still be useful. Farmers' cooperatives, consumer cooperatives, credit unions, and antimonopoly laws are all part of the populist legacy.

Populism took on, but did not win, the struggle to democratize capital on a larger scale. The populist "subtreasury" scheme was superseded by the bootless furor over whether to use the gold standard or the silver standard — so much piffle as an economic argument. By the time the populists' ideas on equitable financing for farmers were finally enacted, in mutant form, in the 1930s, it was too late. Agribusiness, the decades-long centralization of agriculture at the expense of the great mass of farmers, had become the product of farm-credit policies acceptable to the U.S. banking community. As Goodwyn notes, "The end result was a loss of autonomy by millions of Americans on the land."

True, populism failed, or, more accurately, was defeated; corporate capitalism and hierarchical social structures prevailed, and even the dream is largely dead. But the movement had effects then and has echoes still. All power structures are changed by revolts.

Easily the most striking recent example of why we need a populist approach to capital is the S&L debacle — half a trillion bucks of the taxpayers' money to pay for an orgy of greed and stupidity. And, as though that were not enough, now come the banks asking for the same deregulation.

Though populism may be dead, the need for it is not. To hear it so debased by those who have no understanding of it is one of those painful, bone-deep ironies that makes one yearn for Jim Beam. That or a good revolution.

Mother Jones, May/June 1992

HISTORY REPEATS AND
REPEATS AND REPEATS . . .

Two friends, one black, one white.

White: "I am so angry. I am so disgusted. God, what does it take for a black person to get justice in this country?"

Black: "I am so tired of hatred. We did this before. We went through this before. It doesn't help. Nothing helps. I am so tired of hatred. I just called to tell you I love you."

All over the country you can hear people struggling to rationalize that stinking verdict. "There must have been some powerful evidence that exonerated those cops that didn't show on the videotape," they say. The entire trial was televised and covered by the press. There wasn't any evidence that exonerated the cops. A caller to C-SPAN said, "We don't know what all the jurors heard that wasn't on the video. It must have been strong evidence, because they knew this was going to happen if they acquitted. Everybody knew." The Los Angeles Police Department had set aside $1 million for overtime in anticipation of disturbances following the verdict.

But when National Public Radio interviewed one of the jurors, he said, his voice shaking, "If we had known this was going to happen . . . if we had had any idea . . . I don't know . . . we would have considered . . ." That's what you get when you live in Simi Valley, California, in a segregated society. Not a clue.

But we have known since the Kerner Commission report in 1968 what causes riots, and the Rodney King case was a recipe for riot from the beginning. Not since the McDuffie case in Miami that touched off the Liberty City riots have we seen such a textbook case. The social scientists must be pleased to see all their predictive indicators working so well.

One side point: That verdict was an insult to every good cop in America — and there are lots of them.

Now we're supposed to move on to the "on-the-other-hand" phase of this discussion. This is not to condone . . . That does not excuse . . . We deplore the violence . . .

I'd rather skip the platitudes and just look at what's in front of us. There it is. The whole rotting, festering mess produced by poverty, unemployment, illiteracy, drugs, and hopelessness. This country has been in denial about it for years. It didn't get any better while we were treating it with malign neglect. As Mother Willie Mae Ford Smith used to say, "People feel like doesn't nobody care."

139

U.S. Attorney General William Barr actually had the gall to say last week, "What we're seeing in the inner-city communities are essentially the grim harvest of the Great Society." Really? Which parts? Head Start? The Job Corps? Community Action Programs? Model Cities? No, it turns out Barr had in mind "the breakdown of the family structure, largely contributed to by welfare policies." I remember the welfare policy that contributed most to the breakdown of the family: It was the infamous "no-man-in-the-house" rule that forced husbands and fathers to abandon their wives and children so they wouldn't starve. It was not part of the Great Society; it was a legacy of mean-spirited, right-wing racists.

The Great Society programs in fact moved millions of people out of poverty. The programs just didn't last long. They have been either killed or grossly underfunded during the past twelve years.

This riot is a wake-up call to Washington, and to the country. The message is simple: We can't afford *not* to save the inner cities. We either fix it or live with the crime and violence, squalor and lawlessness we are now witnessing in L.A. It can't be contained in "bad" neighborhoods anymore.

Being pathologically optimistic, I don't even think it's all that hard to fix. We don't need to reinvent the wheel or come up with any grand, new, overarching vision. We know which Great Society programs worked and we know what was wrong with ones that didn't. We know what needs to be done and we know a lot about how to do it. I, for one, would like to see some of Jack Kemp's housing ideas tried out.

The one thing we can no longer afford to do is ignore what is happening in the inner cities. P. D. James wrote: "Once you have discovered what is happening, you can't pretend not to know, you can't abdicate responsibility. Knowledge always brings responsibility."

Dallas Times Herald, May 3, 1992

THEY'RE REGULATING
EVERYTHING — PLUS THE
KITSCH IN SYNC

"Several years ago," writes a longtime reader, "when you claimed that the state of Texas was fixing to regulate interior decorators, I thought, 'Oh, that Ivins, she'll say anything for a laugh.'

"But now I read in the papers the state is going to do just that: I promise never to doubt you again."

Well, I should hope not.

In fact, the scheme to regulate inferior desecrators has been kicking around for a long time now — pushed not by a government crazed with power, ready to take over every aspect of our lives, unwilling to let The Free Market work its Adam Smith-ish magic — but by, of course, interior decorators themselves.

Those on the right, who hold that Gummint Regulation hobbling the free market is the root of all evil, need to come study the Texas Legislature to find out how the real world works. Gummint Regulation is almost never imposed from

142

above by a power-crazed government, but is almost always a consequence of some trade or industry begging to be regulated. The purpose, you understand, is not to protect consumers from the malefactors of whatever line of work it is.

It's to protect the folks already in that line of work from other folks who would like to muscle in on the action. Thus it is that the state is brought in to regulate the lawn-sprinkler installers, watch-repairers, barbers, cosmetologists, and a plethora of other toilers and spinners, reapers and sowers, who would just as soon not have any more competition, thank you.

These folks always manage to grandfather themselves into whatever trade it is, exempt from the requirements they lay upon whoever else wants to become an inferior desecrator, lawn-sprinkler installer, or watch repairperson.

The Legislature is apt to go along not only because its committees are presented with endless tales of horror concerning appalling interiors, malfunctioning sprinklers, and watches that never work again, but also because the regulatory programs pay for themselves. Those who wish to be licensed to do whatever-it-is have to cough up enough of a fee to cover the testing and inspection the law mandates. With no tax dollars at stake, the Lege is cheerfully prepared to mandate away.

Rather than wasting our time deploring this set of circumstances, I say we should move with vigor to take advantage of it.

For instance, on the matter of interior decoration, now is the time for all good citizens to come to the aid of minimal good taste. Come with me now to interior decoration land to see what splendid amendments we could all propose.

Felonies:

1. Gold spackles in the ceiling;
2. Lime-green shag carpeting;
3. The dread green-and-purple tile combination in the john.

Hanging offenses:

1. Pictures of dogs playing poker;
2. Elvis on velvet (unless part of an overall kitsch theme);
3. Jesus on velvet.

Misdemeanors:

1. Kitchens done entirely in either harvest gold or avocado green;
2. Red-flock wallpaper;
3. Black walls;
4. The phrase "window treatment";
5. The colors ecru, mauve, and taupe.

Fines:

1. Paintings or statues of sleeping Mexicans;
2. Driftwood lamps;
3. Large, dead, painted fish on the wall;

4. Doilies;
5. Knotty pine;
6. Crocheted toilet-paper-roll covers;
7. Plastic vines on the ceiling of the rec room with little white Christmas lights in them;
8. Round waterbeds;
9. China statues of leprechauns under mushrooms;
10. Painted plaster crabs on wall;
11. Mirror frames with either bows or lace on them;
12. Decals on wall of naked ladies dancing around amid a lot of bubbles;
13. Plaster chicken followed by several plaster chicks on lawn (though all other forms of bad taste on lawn, except those already covered by law, shall be exempt: shrines to Virgin Mary in upended bathtubs on lawn to be encouraged on grounds of charming cultural eccentricity);
14. Blue mirror on dining room table with wax fruit on top;
15. Statues of ladies with clocks in their navels;
16. Statues of naked cherubs (including fountains where the water comes out of the wee-wee);
17. The dread pink-and-black tile combination in the john;
18. Mirrors on ceiling;

19. Brooms with dolls on them so the doll's skirt covers the straw part of the broom;
20. Curtains with scallops *and* fringes;
21. Much more.

Send in your suggestions now, folks. I personally think there should be a subsection in the law for Excess of Good Taste — those rooms done entirely in muted beige, oatmeal, and ecru.

Some citizens want to outlaw aqua: I *like* aqua.

We could perhaps save ourselves a lot of tiresome detail in writing the law by specifying: No More Than One Example of Loving-Hands-at-Home per room. This would prevent all those folks who like cross-stitched samplers saying HOME SWEET HOME from becoming misdemeanants.

Perhaps we could extend this to No More Than One Example of Early Americana Per Room (especially butter churns).

As you can see, we have a lot of populist controversy to get through on this one. Although I am antidoily, I believe clear plastic sofa covers should be exempt. I too once had a white sofa and an untrainable black dog. I now have a grunge-colored sofa. What's more, the cats have taken to using it as a scratching post.

Let me hear from you on these pressing matters. Better yet, write your elected representative. Democracy works!

Dallas Times Herald, May 17, 1992

WIGGY REPUBLICANS

At this point, George Bush's approval rating is lower than the percentage of Americans who believe Elvis is still alive. The Republican party, which has won five out of the last six presidential elections and has held the White House for twenty-eight of the past forty years, appears to be foundering too. And the conservative coalition founded by Barry Goldwater and carried to triumph by Ronald Reagan is cracking up. All in all, the R's are in deep doo-doo.

The Republican party is not a homogeneous outfit, even if it is almost exclusively white. The party spans several classes, from upper to lower-middle. It stretches from Main Street to Wall Street, encompassing complacent, small-town Babbitts and corporate CEO's. It includes fundamentalist Christians and genetically Republican Episcopalians. It is the chosen political vehicle of the antiabortion movement and of a miscellany of other single-issue voters, from the prayer-in-the-schools folks to gun nuts to those who want to unleash Chiang Kai-shek. (Psst. He's *still* dead.) Alas, that splendidly civilized specimen of yesteryear, the liberal Republican, is now extinct.

The guts and the brains of the R party — its energy, its anger, and its ideology — have long flowed from the boiling ferment on the far right. Only the money comes from corporate America. But it's the combination of both forces that yields that strange specimen — the wiggy Republican.

It is in reading the publications of right-wing think tanks and in following the debates in such journals as the *National Review*, the *American Spectator*, *Reason*, and *Human Events* that one begins to understand the degree of disarray on the right. The tumult resembles nothing so much as SDS in the days of its decline: the same interminable arguments over arcane points of ideology, the same disconnection from reality, the same factionalism and ferocious self-righteousness, the same sense of paranoia. Sheesh, any minute now we may see right-wing Weathermen looming over the horizon. Maybe Pat Buchanan will go underground.

The basic split on the right is between those who still believe the Reagan Revolution was a grand triumph and those who are trying to figure out what went wrong. Robert L. Bartley, editor of *The Wall Street Journal*, will serve nicely as a handy example of the camp still insisting that it *was* morning in America and that the whole decade of the 1980s was a roaring success. In his recent book, *The Seven Fat Years*, Bartley once more holds high the banner of supply-side economics, the system that was going to solve the deficit by keeping money tight and cutting taxes.

Never mind that Ronald Reagan also managed to spend $2 trillion on the military to protect us from a crumbling Soviet Union, and spent it on such novel examples of crackpottery as Star Wars, which aggravated the ensuing deficits.

Bartley is undiscouraged by the results and claims that inflation was gone and prosperity reigned for seven fat years, from '82 to '88. He seems entirely unfazed by the news that 60 percent of the new wealth created in that decade went to the wealthiest 1 percent of the people. Right-wing heretic Kevin Phillips, on the other hand, is concerned by precisely that phenomenon and sees in it the political end for the Republican party.

A considerably more wiggy debate is raging elsewhere on the right. Many of you may have thought that "values," the Willie Horton of the '92 campaign, emerged when Dan Quayle fearlessly took on Murphy Brown. But no, the great "values" debate had been raging on the right for months before Quayle discovered it. In this never-never land, no one mentions the fact that, under Reagan, the rich got enormously richer, the poor got poorer, and the middle class shrank. No one cares about the health-insurance disaster, the armies of homeless people in the streets, the crumbling infrastructure, an education system that can't teach, the destruction of the environment, or even deficits the size of small galaxies. Nope, their big worry is Oliver Stone.

You may feel you have missed something here — but yes, Oliver Stone, the guy who makes movies, is whom we're talking about. Stone, you see, is emblematic of the "brooding, gloomy, befouling vapors of Kultursmog, that public-health hazard produced by the politics of the infantile Left and by the conjurings of terrific mountebanks." I quote R. Emmett Tyrrell, editor of the *American Spectator* and a man whose prose style runs from perfervid to frothing-at-the-mouth. Neoliberals, he wrote recently, "put one in mind of nothing so much as a commune of transsexuals who, halfway through their surgical refurbishment, had a change of heart."

David Horowitz, who used to put out *Ramparts* and then moved to the far right, now has his very own think tank. Horowitz, echoing Tyrrell, is also determined to focus on the evils of Hollywood. Faced with an inviting array of real evils — AIDS, drugs, racism, poverty — the right wing has chosen to focus on political correctitude in moviemaking. That this is more than slightly insane seems not to have occurred to anyone on the right.

Another intraconservative fight occupying much time and print is the one over who stood with Pat Buchanan and who didn't — and who will have to forfeit his or her credentials as a result. This fight is not so much ideological as it is pure power struggle. With Buchanan now heir to the title of Conservative Champion, where does that leave Jack Kemp, Bill Bennett, Dan Quayle, Phil Gramm, and all those other politically ambitious conservatives? A festive round of name-calling is in progress on the right. Bennett — who, as we all know, cleaned up the nation's number-one problem as Drug Czar — calls Buchanan the "dark side" of conservatism. I believe Bill would know.

A subfight among right-wingers involves the burning issue of the tariff, which, though it may not be high on your list of Most Burning Issues, absorbs much right-wing passion. This is in part because Roger Milliken, chairman of the South Carolina–based textile firm Milliken & Co., is the sugar daddy of the right wing — and he's a protectionist. Milliken provided seed money for both the *National Review* and the Heritage Foundation as well as backing for Strom Thurmond, Barry Goldwater, Ronald Reagan, Newt Gingrich, and Jack Kemp. As John Judis explained in a *New Republic* article last March, Milliken has had a falling out with the Heritage Foundation over the tariff issue, also known as protectionism v. free trade. Your classic Adam Smith–Milton Friedman conservatives believe in unilateral free trade; your Pat Buchanan types have strayed from the fold here and are advocating protectionism.

If all this seems rather distant from certain gritty realities, like standing in the unemployment line, it is. The underlying problem faced by the Republican Right is that it really doesn't believe in government at all. Ronald Reagan used to go around saying that government was not the solution, government was the problem. It has always seemed odd to me that we would put someone in charge of government who didn't want to run it better but wanted to dismantle it.

We come now to some fairly basic concepts. The founders of this country thought government had six purposes: "to form a more perfect Union, establish justice, insure domestic tranquility, provide for the common defense, promote the general welfare, and secure the blessings of liberty to ourselves and our posterity." Government is just a tool, like a hammer. There's nothing intrinsically good or evil about the hammer; it all depends on what it's used for and the skill with which it is used.

Being antigovernment follows on the belief that there is some other organizing principle in society, and indeed so conservatives believe. They believe in the free market. I think it fair to say they worship the free market, in that they do not question it. That unregulated capitalism has proven to be a disaster — the late nineteenth century comes to mind — doesn't seem to have registered with them. Every example one cites is turned on its head: Your average citizen would say that deregulating the S&Ls was not a terrific idea. Bob Bartley, among others, believes the problem was that S&Ls were not deregulated enough. You think junk bonds were a mistake, that they helped undermine the financial system? You don't understand, the R's will say — junk bonds just had a bad name.

The notion that unregulated capitalism leads to cartels and monopolies is not exclusive to Karl Marx. Its American exponent was Teddy Roosevelt, who had some damn firm evidence. In our more recent run at unregulated capitalism, the results have been equally unappetizing: In addition to paying for the S&L crisis, we face a similar and far more costly crisis in commercial banking. In 1982, most of the major media outlets in the United States were controlled by fifty corporations; by 1987, that was down to twenty-nine corporations. A dozen corporations own three-quarters of the daily newspapers. And so on.

Top executives in this corporate world are united in support of George Bush, who is one of their wholly owned subsidiaries. The Republican Right, from George Will on over, takes a dim view of the president. Will wrote of Bush's last State of the Union address that it was billed as the "defining moment of an administration already 1,100 days old. The administration is sharply defined as an administration without definition. . . . [Bush] said the runaway domestic spending under President Bush must stop. He said the explosion of suffocating regulations that has occurred under President Bush must stop. He is on the losing side of a monologue with himself."

The right wing's fears, hopes, and dreams lie elsewhere. But the money's on Bush. And therein lies the Republican dilemma.

Mother Jones, September/October 1992

CONFUSION, UPROAR, AND UPSET

Yoicks! The Perot-nistas are upon us. Here in Texas, where the vertically impaired billionaire who sounds like a Chihuahua is running ahead of both President George Bush and Bill Clinton in the polls, the Perot-nistas are everywhere. It makes my populist heart beat faster, it does, it does, to watch all those ladies in polyester pantsuits and guys in lime-green leisure suits scouring the countryside for signatures on their petitions, not a natural-fiber snob in the whole herd.

They're organizing themselves, you know. Choosing their own state chairs, setting up their own committees and work shifts. It's almost like . . . well, it's sort of . . . what I mean is, it looks a lot like democracy in action, friends. So naturally the entire Establishment is shitting bricks. Isn't it lovely?

What a splendid year this has been: confusion, uproar, and upset. The three candidates who have enjoyed surges, much to the horror of the Insiders (I'm never exactly sure who I mean by that, but

154

George Will looking as though his hemorrhoids were paining him always comes to mind) are Patrick Buchanan, Jerry Brown, and Ross Perot. What all three have done is crystallize and articulate our discontents and anger. Alas, none of them has put forth much of a program to fix things. Still, it's been great fun to watch the Beltway Boys squirm.

Even My Man George is distressed. He sent for his son George the Younger, called Shrub, to fix his campaign. Shrub Bush told friends his daddy thinks "the speeches are not too good and no one is bringing him any initiatives." One is left with an image of the president sitting in the Oval Office, pounding both fists on his desk like a hungry camper, crying, "Bring me initiatives, bring me initiatives." Twenty-six years in government, and he hasn't a single thought of his own about what might usefully be done to fix things.

Having tried to preempt Bill Clinton's initiative on the Soviet Union and having gotten caught at it, having swiped Clinton's initiative on education and having gotten caught at it, Bush is now reduced to repackaging his own noninitiatives. Thus, we hear from various underlings who solemnly assure us the president is prepared to put $50 million into saving the cities. Same inadequate $50 million already on the books. He named health insurance as top priority in his State of the Union address, but we now hear he will not send any health-insurance legislation to Congress.

Congress itself finally got off its collective duff

and is about to pass the critically needed Spending Limit and Election Reform Act. No fooling this time. No Lucy and the football, where the House passes it but the Senate doesn't or vice versa. But as of this writing, Bush says he will veto it. Jeez, this is depressing.

One seldom sees Bush being an actively bad president — inadequate, hesitant, silly, wrong-headed, short on the vision thing, yes, but not often just dumb and mean like this.

Bush is barely bearable anymore except in his silly mode. In one of his silly moments, he introduced a speech to a Republican fundraiser in Florida by meditating first on how to win. "Let's ask Steinbrenner how the Yanks win. My friend George. By one run." And then on how pleasant it was to go to a strawberry festival and eat short-cake without having to get permission from Congress.

His goofy-guy mode is getting weirder. In addition to tangling himself up in hopeless half-sentences, he now gets his gestures backwards. He'll say, "And the deficit is growing bigger and bigger," while gesturing lower and lower toward the floor. Dave Barry thinks he's gotten better since he stopped taking Halcion, but I think he's had a relapse. During his press conference on his new proposal to provide aid to the former Soviet Union, Bush said, "I will say that I think it is enough and that it's what we ought to do right now — and fight like heck for what we believe in here. And I think it is."

Any meditation on My Man George's health brings us ineluctably to the Veep, who is quietly doing a great deal of damage these days. While Johnny Carson and Jay Leno continue to immortalize his deer-frozen-in-the-headlights reaction to any question more complicated than, "How ya doin'?" the Veeper and his Council on Competitiveness are quietly giving special privileges to corporate buddies. This is the real stuff.

The Progressive, July 1992

NEW HEIGHTS OF PIFFLE

It just gets better and better, doesn't it? The Los Angeles riots may have been a tragedy for L.A., and are indeed indicative of a larger tragedy in this country, but they have inspired our only presidential candidates to new heights of piffle.

Immediately after the verdict in the Rodney King case was announced, George Bush was inspired to say, "The court system has worked. What we need now is calm and respect for the law while we wait for the appeals process to work." No one had bothered to explain to the president that you cannot appeal an acquittal.

Then Dan Quayle contributed his mite by blaming the situation on declining values, for which he fingered sitcom character Murphy Brown. We live in a great nation.

It's now clear that the flag-and-Willie-Horton of the 1992 campaign will be values — a shame, since it used to be a perfectly good word. A trifle amorphous, to be sure, but when you added some modifier — Christian values, humanistic values, family values — at least we were all in the same ballpark as to what we were talking about. Going back to Puritan days, Americans have been fond of sitting around disparaging other people's morals. We could continue to do this for the rest of this political campaign, or we might start talking about how to fix what's wrong with the country.

Meantime, my man H. Ross is stronger than Tabasco, surging into the lead in the polls on the strength of not having proposed one damn thing about how to fix anything. I was enchanted by H. Ross's 1955 letter to the secretary of the navy explaining why he, Ross Perot, did not want to finish his four-year hitch. He was shocked, *shocked,* to find that men in the United States Navy took the Lord's name in vain. Gadzooks! We are shocked, too, of course. What a shattering surprise.

"I have found the Navy to be a fairly Godless organization," wrote Perot. "I do not enjoy the prospect of continuing to stand on the quarterdeck as Officer of the Deck in foreign ports, being subjected to drunken tales of moral emptiness, passing out penicillin pills, and seeing promiscuity on the part of married men.

"I constantly hear the Lord's name taken in vain at all levels. I find it unsatisfying to live, work, and be directed in an atmosphere where taking God's name in vain is a part of the everyday vocabulary. I have observed little in the way of a direct effort to improve a man morally while he is in the Navy or even hold him at his present moral level."

Well, poop, I always counted on the navy for moral uplift myself. Doesn't everyone enlist in the navy for corrective spiritual enlightenment? Where's Mr. Roberts when you need him?

What we have here is a Portrait of the Young Man as a Prig. Comparing the letter Bill Clinton wrote at age twenty-one to the letter Ross Perot wrote at twenty-five is an exercise in the difference between pietistic piffle and genuine moral agony. Young Bill Clinton was clearly tortured by the war in Vietnam — not so much by the prospect of being killed as of having to kill on behalf of a corrupt regime that did not even have the support of its own people. Ross Perot, as he later admitted, did not get along with his commanding officer.

Perot's interest in other people's marital fidelity is beginning to seem more than a little wiggy. He often lectured his employees on the subject in the early days of EDS. In some ways, he did try to help strengthen the families of those who worked for him — he gave stock to wives in their names, took couples out to dinner, held family picnics for employees. But he also demanded total loyalty of his employees and worked them to a point where they almost never saw their families. The definition of an absentee father was someone working for EDS. An absentee father who never took the Lord's name in vain.

While we're all engaged in these weighty debates about Murphy Brown and cursing in the navy, the country continues to unravel, and a good place for serious students of government to watch it do so is at Dan Quayle's very own Council on Competitiveness. Here we see, unobscured by smoke screens of rhetoric, what's wrong with the country. This is where the special interests who have given huge contributions to the Republican party get their payoffs. And what a festive sight it is. Relax the regulations, bend the rules, grant exceptions, pay off the contributors. No shame, no bull.

These are the people bringing you a campaign the centerpiece of which is moral values. Don't you think we should know better than to listen to politicians prating about values?

The Progressive, August 1992

UNITED WE STAND . . . DIVIDED AND DURN PROUD OF IT

Happy July Fourth weekend! I trust you all survived the birthday with limbs intact, and in case your Fourth did not come complete with the requisite Patriotic Address, here's one. And even if it did, here's another. You can't have too many Patriotic Addresses this weekend, especially if you've been subjected to the kind usually given by politicians, those revoltingly saccharine speeches that make the "Up with People!" people sound like a bunch of whiny pessimists.

I love America, in part because, as Marianne Moore once wrote in another context, "It is an honor to witness so much confusion." Ted Morgan is an American who was born a French aristocrat. One reason he decided to become an American is because he so enjoys watching our countrymen confronted with a problem. Me too. We immediately mount horses and charge off in 360 different directions.

How can you not love a nation that holds an

election to decide which Elvis should appear on the stamp in his honor? How can you not love a nation full of people who engage in burning debate over this question, who write passionate letters-to-the-editor in favor of the Young Elvis or the Old Elvis? How can you not love a nation full of mumpish cranks who also write passionate letters-to-the-editor denouncing the whole idea as the veriest hogwash and as yet another Symbol of Our Decay?

A prudent citizen would find it difficult to generalize about 250 million Americans, but I find it irresistible. I love the spunk, common sense, and can-do practicality of so many Americans. I love the terminal common sense of Midwesterners, the distinctly dotty charm of Southerners, and the *Yeeee-Hah!* exuberance of Texans.

I love our national habit of polling ourselves to find out how ignorant we are and our subsequent fits of mortification when we all slap our respective foreheads in alarm because the latest poll shows 62.7 percent of us believe Alexis de Tocqueville never should have divorced Blake Carrington.

It is not the symphony of voices in sweet concert I enjoy, but the cacophany of democracy, the brouhahas and the donnybrooks, the full-throated roar of a free people busy using their right to freedom of speech. Democracy requires rather a large tolerance for confusion and a secret relish for dissent. This is not a good country for those who are fond of unanimity and uniformity.

I love this land, and because I have spent most of my life in the West, I think first of the country here: not just the obvious beauty spots — anyone can go gaga over the Rockies or the Tetons or the Grand Canyon. I also love the Big Bend and the Hill Country of Texas, the red rock country in southern Utah, northern New Mexico, and Louisiana's bayou country. I even love Lubbock, which I must confess is an acquired taste, sort of like anchovies.

The people I admire most in our history are the hell-raisers and the rabble-rousers, the apple-cart upsetters and plain old mumpish eccentrics who just didn't want to be like everybody else. They are the people who made and make the Constitution of the United States a living document — Tom Paine and Clarence Darrow, Mother Jones and Harriet Tubman, Margaret Sanger and Martin Luther King, Jr., Brown of *Brown* v. *the Board of Education*, Joe Hill and Frederick Douglass, Sockless Jerry Simpson and Eleanor Roosevelt, John Henry Faulk and J. Frank Dobie, Saul Alinsky and Ralph Nader.

And I believe every word of the Declaration: I do hold these truths to be self-evident, that all men are created equal, that they are endowed by their Creator with certain unalienable Rights, that among these are Life, Liberty, and the pursuit of Happiness. — That to secure these rights, Governments are instituted among Men, deriving their just powers from the consent of the governed. — That whenever any Form of Government becomes

164

destructive of these ends, it is the Right of the People to alter or to abolish it . . .

Let's celebrate it today, too.

Fort Worth Star-Telegram, July 5, 1992

IN TEXAS, ATTITUDE MAKES UP FOR LACK OF ALTITUDE IN MEN

A colleague from out of state called to inquire, "What *is* it about these Texas runts?" He meant the political runts with an attitude. "I'm talking about Ross Perot, Claytie Williams, John Tower, Bill Clements. What *is* it with these people?"

I explained that it is not easy to be a short, male Texan. If you can't be a long, tall Texan, our tradition calls for you to weigh in with at least 130 pounds of bad attitude to make up for it.

Nor is the phenomenon limited to Republicans and right-wingers. For example, both Jim Hightower and Sam Rayburn could be listed as runts with attitude, except that, since they're Democrats and thus politically correct, we would have to call them vertically impaired, or possibly differently abled height-wise.

Several readers have written to object to my having referred to Ross Perot as a Chihuahua. Actually, this was not intended as a reference to his size, or even to the size of his ears. It was his voice I had in mind; he yaps.

Now, my readers have pointed out that Perot's physical characteristics, including his stature or lack of it, have nothing to do with his qualifications for the presidency, with which I heartily concur. I was merely attempting a descriptive analogy. He does sound like a Chihuahua. Under no circumstances would I suggest that this bars him from the presidency.

Harry Truman also sounded like a yapping dog, but it had no effect on his presidency.

Well, much as I have enjoyed playing with Perot, whom I actually rather like, I'm afraid it's time to point out a few of his failings beyond Bad Haircut.

Ross Perot is a liar. It's really quite striking and leaves me with a certain respect for professional politicians, who lie with such artistry, such deniability, such masterful phraseology that they can always deny their denials later on.

Perot lies the way Henry Kissinger used to lie but without Kissinger's air of grave, weighty authority. Perot just flat-out lies. What's more, when he lies, he accuses everyone else of lying. He never said this; he never said that; he never said the other. They're making it all up. They're all liars.

They're all out to get him. You should check on their reputations (hint, hint).

Some bidness expert explained the other day that Perot lies like that because he's an entrepreneur, and those guys are always out on such limbs that they have to lie. It was a new theory to me.

Perot is seriously into paranoid, right-wing conspiracy theories. Actually, this is not news. We've known this about him for years. But now we have to do some serious thinking about what it means to have a president whose grip on reality is both infirm and elastic.

By now your humble servants in the ink trade have documented Perot's connections to Lyndon LaRouche-ites, Christic Institute fantasists, Ollie North at his wiggiest (Perot says Ollie is lying, Ollie made it all up, no such thing ever happened), and various oddball spinoffs of the there-are-still-POW's-in-Asia theory.

Ross Perot spies on people. Perot keeps saying he didn't know anything about instances of EDS employees being spied on. Maybe so. But he hired a P.I. to snoop on Senator Warren Rudman of New Hampshire, a P.I. to snoop on some of the *contra* stuff, sent his own company lawyer and two pilots to check into parts of the October Surprise scenario, offered to show supposedly incriminating photos to the *Star-Telegram* publisher and a *Washington Post* reporter.

I don't like the way the guy plays. If he can't have it all his way, he takes his ball and goes home. Whether it's the promise of a big donation to a Dallas charity or the case of General Motors, Perot's been a bully and a quitter. And no matter whom he crosses or who crosses him, his story is always the same: He's completely in the right and the other guy's completely in the wrong.

I think it is a damned lousy idea to vote for

anyone who's paying for his own campaign. You've all heard me complain for however long you might have been reading this column about the way we finance elections in this country. It's sorry, it's sleazy, and it's got to stop.

But the biggest loophole in the campaign law right now is that it puts a one-thousand-dollar limit on contributions to campaigns for federal office *unless it's your own campaign.*

Well, dammit, we already know this system is giving us a government of the special interests, by the special interests, and for the special interests. The players in politics all have or have access to big money. That's what's wrong with the government of this country.

OK, so maybe we figured that at least Perot wouldn't owe anything to the usual chorus of special interests. I mean, if it was all his money, maybe he'd actually work for *us.*

But look, in the first place, it's bad enough the extent to which rich people and their bought lackeys already run this country. Why make it worse?

In the second place, look at Perot's proposals. He, like Bush, favors a cut in the capital-gains tax: That's the move that helps rich people. He also wants to take away Congress's power to levy taxes. In a speech to the National Press Club, he proposed this startling notion and said, "You say, 'Well, that means a constitutional amendment.' Fine."

I don't like people who think it's fine, chop-chop, no big deal, to change the Constitution of this country. I think Madison and Jefferson and Adams and all those guys were wiser than Ross Perot. I think they put the right to tax in the branch of government closest to the people for good reasons. Perot says he wants to throw out the current tax system and start with a blank piece of paper. But he hasn't said what he wants to write on it. Don't you people think issues aren't important?

Ronnie Dugger has pointed out that since presidents have already ripped up one of the major constitutional powers of Congress — to declare war — and Perot wants to remove another, that would leave Congress with just one important power: to spend. Except that Perot wants the right to veto any appropriation passed by Congress.

Let's see, that would give him war, peace, taxes, spending. Can anyone think of anything else he'd need to be our first dictator?

Fort Worth Star-Telegram, July 9, 1992

THE NONPROFESSIONAL
FINDS OUT POLITICS ISN'T
AS EASY AS IT LOOKS

Look, Ross Perot knows as much about running for public office as a hog knows about Sunday. So if he had a lick of sense he would have listened to the people who do know. He didn't.

Then we get to the question of desire. As coaches keep telling their players, the team that wins is the team that wants it most. The flattering version of this is "fire in the belly." The negative spin, as we say in politics, is raw, unquenchable ambition. The kind that made George Bush say, "I will do anything to win." The kind that put Bill Clinton in this race when George Bush looked unbeatable and kept Clinton there when he was getting beaten bloody. Perot would prefer to have us believe that he is not eaten up with the kind of clawing, persevering ambition it takes to win. But a coach would say he just didn't have enough want-to.

Perot's supporters, who put together one of the most effective and spontaneous grass-roots movements in my political memory, are entitled to feel let down and, if they want to, betrayed. But I suspect they like their man enough to take him at his word: that he's doing what he thinks is best for the country.

Perot denied today that he had said the campaign wasn't fun anymore — but he's denied a lot of things he actually said in the course of his would-be candidacy. I suspect that was just the problem. Politics is a lot of fun when you start. You announce, and bands play and balloons come down and all your friends cheer. And then it all turns into the nasty, dirty, hardball game it really is and it is no fun at all. That's why we're all right to suspect that politicians are slightly abnormal to put up with it. Politics looks easy from the outside: That's why guys like Perot think they can do it, and do it without all the consultants and folderol and shuckin' and jivin' you have to do to get elected. He's learned better.

The classic example was Perot's speech to the NAACP. Perot was genuinely outraged and pained that anyone would construe a racist tinge to that speech. The media did sound silly trying to say the problem was his use of the phrase "you people" when addressing a black audience. It's a perfectly reasonable phrase, not unlike "y'all." But the speech itself was enough to make any practicing politician wince: You don't go in front of a black audience and try to prove your empathy by telling stories about how kind your daddy was to the darkies who worked for him, helping them get out

172

of jail, for God's sake. Or that your mama used to feed all the black hobos who came by. What that does is leave the audience with the impression that the only blacks you ever knew when you were growing up wound up in jail every Saturday night or were shiftless hobos.

When Perot committed gaffes like that — the NAACP was the biggest, but not the only one — he would then blame it on the media being unfair, for not putting the right interpretation on what he said or meant to say, and he would then attempt to instruct or lecture the press on how we were to interpret him. It was painful to watch. When you run for public office, you don't get to decide what other people think of you.

Watching someone without political skills try to run for public office sure as hell increased my respect for political skills, including the artful evasion, always so preferable to the outright lie.

Myself, I always kind of liked Ross Perot. By the time he announced he wouldn't run today, he sure had convinced me he shouldn't.

Fort Worth Star-Telegram, July 17, 1992

173

THE BEST OF THE CONVENTION: UNCONVENTIONAL DELEGATES

So humiliating. I've flunked Media Cynicism 101 again. I just love political conventions. The 14,999 other media people here spent all week bitching because this was such a boring convention: no fights, no news, no action, until, of course, Ross decided to prove he's all hawk and no spit.

My favorite stuff is what the delegates dream up on their own. One hand-lettered sign Thursday night read, YOU'RE NO AL GORE EITHER, DAN. During Jimmy Carter's speech, a delegate held up a sign that said, AMY NEVER OWNED AN S&L. The delegation from Idaho, where they take spuds seriously, put up flash cards that spelled out I-D-A-H-O, with one guy standing at the end with a little *e*. (Surely we can count on the R's from Idaho to come up with a good Quayle spelling jest of their own in Houston next month.) Indiana introduced itself during roll call as "The home of the next retired vice president of the United States." The Texas delegation took revenge on its dumpy hostel by hanging a HOTEL HELL banner out the front windows. Television camera guys took to wearing BLAME IT ON THE MEDIA T-shirts.

The professional wordmeisters didn't do badly either. The R's spin doctor, Roger Ailes, was sparring with the D's Bob Shrum on a late-night chat show. "Well," said Ailes, "Clinton certainly went for the dysfunctional-family vote."

"Oh," replied Shrum, "do you really think the Reagans will vote for him?" (Come to think of it, the Reagans' kids probably will.)

Clinton's speech, clearly written by a committee, was a masterful political speech, even if it did nothing for the reputation of the English language. Gore's speech, on the other hand, was pure political poetry. When he started on the tale of his son's accident, I was afraid we were in for a bad case of mawkish exploitation of personal tragedy. But then he turned it into a stunning political metaphor.

On the other hand, no one's ever going to be able to claim that the R's have the lock on vomitinously maudlin biographical films again. Except for the priceless footage of young Bill Clinton shaking hands with JFK, those bio films were the most shamelessly sentimental tripe we've had to suffer through since the Nancy-and-Ronnie-Wander-Through-the-Woods film at the Dallas convention in '84.

Best single line of the night was Gore's assertion, "Hillary Clinton and Tipper Gore have done more for children in the past twelve years than the two men who were sitting in the White House have done in their lifetimes."

Perot's bombshell caught the R spinners so off-guard, they were still trashing him as his news conference started. They went into reverse so fast it was hysterical: In a twinkling he went from Dangerous Fascist Creep to Great American Who Has Changed the Political Landscape. You have to admire a spinner who can do that with a straight face.

Speaking of political professionalism, did you notice Jesse Jackson's etiquette lesson for Jerry Brown? Jackson's graceful and gracious endorsement of Clinton (who had, as they say in the streets, "dissed" Jackson before his own Rainbow Coalition) as much as said to Brown, "Look, stupid, here's how you're supposed to handle these things."

I've started keeping lists: People I See and Kiss Once Every Four Years at Political Conventions. People I See and Kiss at Conventions Whose Names I Have Forgotten. People I See and Kiss at Conventions Whose Names I Never Knew. There are some real joys to longevity.

Fort Worth Star-Telegram, July 19, 1992

176

GOP SEEMS TO VALUE UGLY BUT TRADITIONAL TACTIC OF US VS. THEM

In the face of increasingly bad economic news, Bush and the Republicans have increasingly pitched the re-election campaign on "family values," a nebulous phrase that the GOP hopes connotes a social permissiveness on the part of Democrats, especially the party's support for homosexual rights.
— **News story, *Houston Chronicle*, July 29**

The *Chronk*'s analysis is conventional wisdom already. The Republicans are going to run against gays. Last time out, they used Willie Horton and our fear of black criminals to take our minds off the Iran-*contra* scandal, the S&L crisis, the faltering economy, and the whole greedfest of the eighties.

This time it's homosexuals, dying by the hundreds of thousands of a terrible disease, who get to be "Them."

It seems to me the question here is not whether

177

we approve of gay people, but what we make of a political party willing to whip up hatred against a minority group for partisan political gain. There is certainly a moral question involved.

This "social-issues" game has been going on since the late 1960s, when running against unpopular "life-styles," specifically long-haired, dope-smoking kids, proved to be a big hit. Come to think of it, the game is a lot older than that. In the late nineteenth century, running against "rum, Romanism, and rebellion" was the code phrase for much-despised Catholic immigrants.

Old dog still hunts. Get people all excited about some perceived menace from an unpopular group and maybe they won't notice the unemployment rate, maybe they'll forget that the richest 1 percent of the people got sixty percent of the new wealth in the eighties, maybe they'll overlook the exemptions carved out for the big donors to the Republican party by Dan Quayle's Council on Competitiveness.

In an attempt to keep our collective eye on the shell with the pea under it, let's take another look at Ross Perot's deficit-reduction plan, with the help of Jamie Galbraith, the Texas economist (it runs in his family). The Texas Galbraith raises what is probably the most important question to be asked about Perot's plan to balance the federal budget in five years: Is this really a right and proper goal?

Perot himself, before he dropped out of the race, predicted it would take twelve years to balance the budget and noted several times that it had to be done slowly and carefully in order not to hurt the economy. Because this is the fact of life: When you raise taxes and cut government spending, it slows economic growth.

Galbraith has run the numbers on the Perot plan, which is still short of details, and this is his conclusion:

> I calculate that real economic growth, presently predicted at 3 percent each year, would fall below 2 percent by 1996, and virtually to zero by 1998. Unemployment would rise steadily, undermining the hoped-for expenditure savings. And with slower growth, the economy will be smaller every year than presently predicted, until by 1998 there would be a gap of just about $1 trillion below current projection for GDP [Gross Domestic Product, slightly different technically from the more familiar numbers in the old Gross National Product]. Tax revenues would fall in proportion — by nearly $200 billion. In the end, the deficit would scarcely be smaller than if no plan were tried at all!

Galbraith goes on to say there are ways around this scenario. You could balance the negative effect of harsh budget cuts with a massive export program, based partly on an industrial policy that was the key to Perot's campaign and is also part of Clinton's economic plan. But the Perot plan does not address that question and appears to rely on monetary policy alone to keep growth going. This is the same scheme that has so notably not been working under George Bush.

Galbraith's critique includes some praise for the Perot plan.

"The Perot plan is bold. It contains a needed public investment program and cuts of unneeded defense spending. The gas tax is a serious proposal. So is the idea of taxing more of Social Security income. So is a higher top-bracket income tax rate. An incremental investment tax credit has respected backers, as well as opponents."

But Galbraith also describes the Perot plan's 10 percent across-the-board reduction in government spending as "classic smoke-and-mirrors." And he adds, "Strikingly, the plan provides tax relief to one group: rich people seeking to realize capital gains. There is no reputable economic case for this measure, and scant evidence that past capital gains cuts did any good. Recent studies even suggest that about half of realized capital gains are actually consumed, not reinvested, so that this break, even when restricted to long-term stock holdings, amounts to a tax preference for high living. This is an especially strange inclusion in a plan so full of sacrifice from everyone else."

Fort Worth Star-Telegram, July 30, 1992

CAMPAIGN DIRT'S FLYING HIGH, HITTING WAY BELOW THE BELT

"We've never said that he's a philandering, pot-smoking draft dodger," said George Bush's campaign political director.

"The way you just did?" asked a *New York Times* reporter.

"The way I just did," replied the campaign official.

What an attractive little campaign document that was, the Bush press release put out by his campaign Sunday, the one headlined, SNIVELING HYPOCRITICAL DEMOCRATS: STAND UP AND BE COUNTED. ON SECOND THOUGHT, SHUT UP AND SIT DOWN!

The press release, in which Democratic nominee Bill Clinton is referred to throughout as "Slick Willie," has a tasteful, high-minded tone.

The quotes are, according to the Bush campaign, around phrases used either by Clinton or by people in his campaign.

You feel like a "one-man landfill?" No, Willie, it's not those Wendy's burgers, or Dunkin' Donuts or even those scrumptious home-baked cookies. It's that Alka-Seltzer feeling you get when you're the leader of the "garbage load."

We respectfully request you and your fellow Democrat sniveling hypocrites read our lips: SHUT UP AND SIT DOWN so we can get back to more highlights of the Clinton record. If we're at your "bellybutton," it feels like Mount Everest compared to your lower-than-a-snake's-belly campaign.

The press release goes on to ask, "Which campaign had to spend thousands of tax-payer dollars on private investigators to fend off 'bimbo eruptions'?"

That question was said to be justified because presidential candidates get federal money for their election campaigns after the nominating conventions and because Betsey Wright, a Clinton campaign aide, told *The Washington Post* quite some time ago that she was having to deal with "bimbo eruptions" caused by women claiming they had had extramarital affairs with Clinton after the Gennifer Flowers story broke.

Just last week Bush said again that the candidates' personal lives are "off-limits" and that he had ordered his campaign to stay away from them.

I'm sure we'd all like to thank the Bush campaign for this deft, delicate example of light-handed political humor. For this thoughtful response to the nation's economic problems, housing crisis, and health-insurance mess, we are all profoundly grateful.

Actually, George Bush did say something in response to a Clinton proposal Sunday: He said Clinton's proposal will give us a "health-care system that will combine the efficiency of the House post office with the compassion of the KGB."

Mr. Bush does not have a health-care proposal.

Whew. This one is sliding into the gutter faster than anyone had counted on. I've watched sheriff's races in Potter County with more dignity than this. The singularly ugly press release put out by the Bush campaign was, according to the Bush campaign, justified by what they said was Clinton's having called Bush a tax evader because Bush keeps a voting address at a Houston hotel and so does not have to pay an income tax in Maine.

The "tax evader" charge was actually made a few months ago in the comic strip Doonesbury and was, you will recall, turned to good use by our state comptroller, John Sharp, who cheerfully sold "Honorary Texan" certificates to out-of-staters looking for a similar tax break.

Personally, I think that what all this proves is that when you want to use political humor against an opponent, it's best to get someone funny to write it.

Fort Worth Star-Telegram, August 4, 1992

IGNORANCE EPIDEMIC THREATENS IN TEXAS DURING AIDS CRISIS

What is this? Dog days of August? Full moon? Stars in strange alignment?

There is this outbreak of nuttiness all over the state about AIDS. We are in the tenth year of the AIDS epidemic.

We all know there are still slope-browed, egg-sucking ridge-runners out in the hills who believe that only homosexuals get AIDS and that it serves them right. But most of us long ago accepted the fact that this virus doesn't give a damn what your sexual preference is.

AIDS started in Africa as a disease sexually transmitted by heterosexuals, and its fastest growth rate in this country is now among teenagers and women. So far, the only group spared by sexual preference is lesbians, a fact that must give some pause to those who believe that it is all God's plan. Ignorance and fear are still the most important factors in the spread of AIDS, but we have long since come to expect our public officials to be responsible about the epidemic. But nooooo, not in Texas.

Leaping like the virus itself from San Antonio to Houston to Corpus Christi, we are having a merry little round of gay-bashing spread by the resident buffoons on the city councils of those fair towns. It started in San Antone, the town that gave us Benny Eureste and Henry Van Archer as standards of civic intelligence.

Dr. Fernando Guerra, director of the city's Metropolitan Health District, was understandably upset when the Bexar County AIDS Consortium, the umbrella funding group for the area, decided to cut $93,000 from a $119,000 grant to the health district for AIDS management services. The consortium wanted to put the money into other organizations doing front-line work with AIDS patients. Dr. Guerra told the *San Antonio Express-News* he thought the decision was affected by the fact that members of the consortium who have the AIDS virus might be suffering from impaired judgment caused by AIDS-related conditions, possibly even dementia.

Dr. Guerra, who knows better, promptly apologized for the remarks. The funding cut may or may not have been bad judgment, but as the citizens of Texas know, bad judgment on the part of our leaders is not limited to those with the human immunodeficiency virus.

But then Councilman Weir Labatt decided to jump in by attacking those with AIDS. "I'm real tired of the AIDS community thinking there's something special about them," he said.

Labatt went on to say: "The reason they have AIDS is their lifestyle — the majority of them being drug IV users or having engaged in male-to-male intercourse. The only people they should be upset at are themselves. I suggest they retract their anger. If the local AIDS community is always making noise, I'd rather see the money used in some other area and not go to AIDS patients."

Die quietly, that's his motto; no raging against the dying of the light for Councilman Labatt.

Now in Houston, Councilman John Goodner, a blustery fellow, up and opined that money being spent on AIDS was going down a one-way tube and that if we'd quarantined these people to begin with, we wouldn't have a problem.

I don't know what it is about people dying of AIDS, but they seem to think they have a serious problem. As Labatt noted, they do make noise. One Houston AIDS activist was arrested on a charge of aggravated assault for demonstrating against Goodner, which just goes to show how much Houston has to learn from Dallas.

At Dallas City Council meetings, what Houston considers aggravated assault is considered normal citizen input and happens every week. And people think Dallas is an uptight town.

Meanwhile, down in Corpus, Councilman Leo Guerrero got into a fight about whether to charge a buck a head to let folks into Bayfest, the annual civic fandangle. He said on a radio show that it would help keep out undesirables like drunks and homosexuals.

You will not be amazed to learn that Corpus gays made noise. So then Guerrero, who is pretty noisy himself, launched into a soliloquy about gays picking up kids on the Seawall and the police were called in to confirm that such things have been known to happen somewhere in the Shining City by the Sea, and with that everyone got mad just in time for Bayfest, which upset the Junior League.

So next there was a huge demonstration at the City Council meeting with local activists raising hell and a counterdemonstration by kids from what used to be the late Brother Lester Roloff's home, he who added such je ne sais quoi to life in Corpus. The kids, who wore Guerrero T-shirts, kept raising their Bibles in unison, and all in all it was much more entertaining than the average City Council meeting.

Far be it from me to discourage the excellent Texas tradition of lunacy in local government. Long may it continue to add color and entertainment to our civic life. And of course I wish the gay militant groups like ACT-UP and Queer Nation still had the astonishing dignity and theatrical impact of their early demonstrations. But then, it's hard to maintain continuity in an organization when the leadership keeps dying.

I'm afraid we are all going to have to recognize and deal with the quality that distinguishes those with AIDS — desperation. Many of these dying people have been spat on all their lives, called "queer" from the time they were ten, been beaten up with some frequency, and now they're dying before they're thirty from a disease their government keeps trying to ignore.

For some reason, they don't think they have a lot left to lose.

Fort Worth Star-Telegram, August 13, 1992

NOTES FROM ANOTHER COUNTRY

Nothing like a Republican convention to drive you screaming back into the arms of the Democrats. Especially this convention. The elders of the press corps kept muttering they hadn't seen anything like it since the Goldwater convention in '64. True, the Republicans spent much of their time peddling fear and loathing, but it was more silly than scary, like watching people dressed in bad Halloween werewolf costumes. During the buildup to the convention, the most cockeyed optimists among the Democrats were in hopes the Republicans would tear themselves apart over abortion. No need. The party was dead meat on arrival.

I am a cautious political bettor. It's silly to put money down any closer than six weeks out from Election Day, and one should never underestimate the ability of the Democrats to screw up. But the Republicans have nothing going for them, and nothing they can try works. They got a three-point bounce out of their convention. The in-depth polling shows the great majority of the public didn't care for the gay-bashing, didn't care for the feminist-bashing, didn't care for the Hillary-bashing, and thought the whole exercise was too negative. It was.

The most surprising aspect of the convention was George Bush, and the surprise was — no surprises, not even a mini-idea. His own advisers were pushing the line that his big speech would finally, at long last, answer all the questions — how to get out of the recession, what the domestic agenda should be, and what his vision thing actually is. They even promised that after four long years we would learn who the hell he is and what he really believes. We got nothing.

On the economy, one more time, he pushed a capital-gains tax cut. There is little historical evidence that a cap-gains cut stimulates the economy, and recent studies by academic economists (as opposed to the political kind) show that half of realized capital gains go straight into consumption. It's the dumbest kind of tax subsidy to conspicuous consumption you can try.

You can argue, as both Paul Tsongas and Bill Clinton do, that a targeted capital-gains cut would be beneficial. Bush not only wants the cut with no strings, he's even arguing for a cut on past investments, which is nothing but a windfall for richies.

The confabulation in Houston was not, however, without its charms. I loved Ronald Reagan's speech — especially the line about Thomas Jefferson. Until it occurred to me to wonder what would have happened if Jefferson, surely the finest intellect this soil has ever produced, actually did meet Reagan. Imagine the conversation:

"Ignorance is preferable to error; and he is less remote from the truth who believes nothing, than he who believes what is wrong."

"Well. Make my day."

(Such ruminations may be a consequence of the brain damage caused by listening to Republicans bloviate for hours on end. In the line of journalistic duty, I attended the God and Country Rally featuring Phyllis Schlafly, Pat Robertson, and Pat Boone, and am filing a worker's compensation claim against *The Nation*.)

Many people did not care for Pat Buchanan's speech; it probably sounded better in the original German.

No one could decide whether Phil Gramm or Pat Robertson made the worst speech of the convention, perhaps because no one listened to them.

In trying to determine just how far to the right the G.O.P.'s loony wing will go, it's worth noting how Pat Robertson, past and possibly future G.O.P. presidential candidate, is fighting Iowa's proposed equal-rights amendment. Pat says feminism "encourages women to leave their husbands, kill their children, practice witchcraft, destroy capitalism, and become lesbians."

Listening to George Bush, toward the end of his speech, read the poetry written by Ray Price with the gestures scripted by speech coach Roger

Ailes, I was struck anew by the elaborate charade of emperor's clothing in which the American press is so supinely complicit. Bush has no more sense of poetry than he does of grammar. After the speech there was much division in the pundit corps over whether Bush had just "hit it out of the park" (both sports and war metaphors were much in vogue) or whether we had just heard a load of nasty political drivel without a single redeeming idea. But all hands were solemnly pretending we had just heard George Bush, the nation's most incoherent speaker, stand up and make a fifty-eight-minute political address.

George Bush without a TelePrompTer can scarcely produce an intelligible sentence. I've been listening to him since 1966 and must confess to a secret fondness for his verbal dyslexia. Hearing him has the charm and suspense of those old adventure-movie serials: Will this man ever fight his way out of this sentence alive? As he flops from one syntactical Waterloo to the next, ever in the verbless mode, in search of the long-lost predicate, or even a subject, you find yourself struggling with him, rooting for him. What is this man actually trying to say? What could he possibly mean? Hold it, I think I see it!

Imagine, for a mad moment, George Bush in the British Parliament, where the members are not only fluent in English but expected to think on their feet as well. I am told that public policy is often hammered out in the exchange of thought there. How would anyone ever figure out what

Bush thinks? This is not a matter of grammar: Anyone who has ever heard some canny country legislator fracture the language while making his point knows clarity is not synonymous with syntax. The fact is that unless someone else writes a speech for him, the president of the United States sounds like a borderline moron. But the media sit around pretending that he can actually talk — can convince, inspire, and lead us.

We have long been accustomed to hearing Republicans exploit racial fears, usually by talking about crime. The "family-values" issue is a more subtle exploitation of the doubt, confusion, and guilt felt by American women. Women are receiving so many conflicting messages from this society that no matter what choices we make, or more often, what roles necessity forces on us — work, family, or the difficult combination of both — we all feel guilty about what we're doing. It's quite true that full-time homemakers resent the condescension in remarks like Hillary Clinton's "What did you expect me to do, stay home and bake cookies?" But this is a society in which people's worth is judged by how much money they make, and the esteem in which our society holds wives and mothers is reflected in their salaries.

For a political party that has consistently opposed every effort to build a support network for working mothers to then condemn and guilt-trip them is despicable. Natal leave, parental leave, day care — the whole complex of programs that exist in other industrialized nations to help working mothers does not exist here, thanks to the Republican party. Most women in this country work because they have to. Most are still stuck in the pink-collar ghettos of sales personnel, clerical personnel, and waitressing. Clerical workers are in a particular bind as more and more corporations replace them with "temporary workers" in order to avoid having to pay health and retirement benefits.

The gay-bashing at the convention would have been offensive even without the AIDS epidemic. Have they no shame, at long last, have they no shame? I watched delegates who are the mothers of gay sons sit there and listen without protest. I don't know what it says about their family values.

I'm not even sure why any of this was discussed at the political convention, except that the R's clearly see political gain in it. The Constitution says the purpose of our government is "to form a more perfect Union, establish justice, insure domestic tranquility, provide for the common defense, promote the general welfare, and secure the blessings of liberty to ourselves and our prosperity." The president is nowhere designated in the Constitution as arbiter of our sexual morals.

Trying to figure out from whence and why came the nastiness at that convention, I found two sources.

There are lots of nice Republicans in this world, perfectly decent, quite bright people. When Peggy Noonan, Reagan's speech writer, covered the Democratic convention for *Newsweek*, she wrote:

"There was much talk of unity, but what I saw was the pretty homogenized gathering of one of the great parties of an increasingly homogenized country — a country that has been ironed out, no lumps and wrinkles and grass stains, a country in which we are becoming all alike, sophisticated, Gapped, linened and Lancômed." It occurred to me that Noonan not only did not attend the same Democratic convention I did, she does not live in the same country I do.

Turns out she lives in East Hampton, Long Island, which may account for it. Despite having lost her job at the White House a few years ago, she does not seem to have spent any time in the unemployment line. In her country, people aren't worried about their jobs, they aren't caught in hideous health-insurance binds, they aren't watching their standard of living slip slowly down, their hopes for a home slip slowly away, their dreams for the future dwindle. It's another country, the country of those who are Doing Well.

The second source of the nastiness is cynical political professionals pushing divisiveness for political reasons, exploiting fear and bigotry because it works. Old dog. Still hunts.

The professionals around Bush seem, like the man himself, not to believe in much of anything except their own entitlement to power. They are not the true believers of the Reagan years, nor even like the angry lower-middle-class Nixonites feeling snubbed by the Eastern Establishment. Too many years, too many limousines. They're out of touch with the country and fighting like piranhas not for ideas or any vision of a better America — they're fighting to keep their limousines.

The Nation, September 14, 1992

WHEN CLINTON TALKS, PEOPLE LISTEN — AND VICE VERSA

On the Clinton bus, Corsicana — It is a show, and a good one at that. I'd recommend it for everyone, regardless of political persuasion, who enjoys vintage American politics.

Our political life is now so dominated by television that it's wonderfully pleasant to be able to wander down to the courthouse — or the mall — in your own hometown to hear and see the guy who wants to be president while he's out there sweating in the sun with everyone else.

That the entire show is carefully orchestrated for television is just one of the facts of contemporary life.

Clinton is an exceptionally good campaigner. I make this observation in the same spirit in which one would note that Joe Montana is an artist on the football field, even if one were a Cowboys fan. What is, is. The "liberal media" is not inventing Clinton.

As a campaigner, Clinton has great stamina. He

tends to get stronger as the day goes on. He blends gentle ridicule of the whole Bush era with a "We-can-do-it" pitch that is actually classic Reagan. We're the optimists; they're the pessimists.

He has a standard litany of what he plans to do if elected. To my surprise, the one that crowds like most is the national-service idea. Clinton wants to set up a national college trust fund, so any American can get a loan to go to college. Then, he emphasizes that the student will have to pay back the loan, either with a small percentage of his or her earnings after graduation, or by giving two years to public service — as a teacher, as a cop, working with inner-city kids, helping old folks.

As the list goes on, the applause swells. "We can rebuild this country. We can save our cities. We can do it. We can!"

Clinton and Al Gore have a lot of material to work with, given Bush's record, his dingbat mode and latest goofy proposals. Both men needle the president constantly and are rapidly turning the "family-values" convention to their own advantage. Meanwhile, the Bush team, now under Jim Baker, is already quicker at responding and has now dropped family values.

Bush probably made a mistake when he told the evangelical crowd in Dallas last weekend that the Democrats left G-O-D out of their platform (that was before Baker mixed "family values").

An Episcopalian really should know better than to try to out-Bible a couple of Baptist boys. Both Clinton and Gore can quote Scripture to a fare-thee-well, but the ever-magisterial Barbara Jordan, daughter of a Baptist preacher, used it most witheringly at the enormous rally in Austin (best guess, twenty thousand). "Everyone who calleth to me, 'Lord, Lord,' will not get in. Who will get in? Those who do the Lord's work."

Much of the Texas tour, viewed as a whole, is an exercise in inoculation.

The Clinton campaign fully expects Bush to go on television with massive negative buys. In Texas, two obvious targets are guns and gays. If past Republican performance is a reliable indicator, the gay-bashing will be done below radar, on radio.

Clinton tried to defuse the gun issue (he supports the Brady bill, the seven-day hold on gun purchases) by citing Ronald Reagan's support for the Brady bill and touting it as a common-sense measure to help law enforcement.

The Republicans' Texas attack plan, titled "September Storm," contains a memorable wincer. The R's refer to the political operatives with whom they plan to flood East Texas as "Stormtroopers." You don't have to be Jewish to flinch at that lack of historical sensitivity.

Energy, stamina, and joy are key factors that make Clinton such an effective campaigner. Of pols I have watched, he is most like Hubert Humphrey and Ralph Yarborough. He loves doing this. He gets energy from people.

A lot of politicians, Lloyd Bentsen for example, move through crowds smiling and shaking hands. But the smile never reaches their eyes. You can tell they'd much rather be back in Washington cutting deals with other powerful people. In his book *What It Takes: The Way to the White House*, writer Richard Ben Cramer suggests that Bush despises politics, considers it a dirty business, and consequently believes anything is permitted.

The different thing about Clinton is that he listens to people as he moves among them. Humphrey and Yarborough were always talking. Clinton listens and remembers and repeats the stories he hears.

I have read several of the poetic effusions produced by my journalistic colleagues about Clinton's bus tours and laughed. On Thursday evening, in the late dusk, moving among the thousands gathered on the old suspension bridge over the Brazos in Waco, I realized why so many of us wax poetic about these scenes.

It's not Clinton who's so wonderful. It's America.

Fort Worth Star-Telegram, August 30, 1992

SPEAKING OF VALUES, HERE'S SOMEONE WHO TOOK ACTION

"I will never let politics interfere with a foreign policy decision."
— **George Bush, August 20, 1992, Houston**

"We're proud to do this."
— **George Bush, September 3, 1992, Fort Worth, announcing the reversal of a ten-year policy against selling advanced jet fighters to Taiwan**

Possible explanation for the above: "Ours is a great state, and we don't like limits of any kind. Ricky Clunn is one of the great bass fishermen. He's a Texas young guy, and he's a very competitive fisherman, and he talked about learning to fish wading in the creeks behind his dad. He, in his underwear, went wading in the creeks behind his father, and he said — as a fisherman he said — it's great to grow up in a country with no limits." — George Bush, February 28, 1992, Houston

On the other hand, maybe it's not an explanation. Decoding Bush is becoming so exhausting that I turned to Dan Quayle this weekend for relief, thus stumbling across another of the defining moments of the '92 campaign. This was Quayle's speech pitting the values of Huntington, Indiana, one of his hometowns (the other being Phoenix, Arizona), against those of Hollywood, California. The tinny, inauthentic sound of Quayle as Moral Authority has to have been heard to be properly appreciated, but I shall do my best to reproduce the gist.

It seems "They," in Hollywood, do not understand Huntington, Indiana. "They" do not appreciate Huntington. "They" do not like Huntington.

One's mind does tend to wander during a Quayle speech. Do you suppose people in Hollywood actually do spend a lot of mental and emotional energy thinking about Huntington, Indiana? Should the good citizens of Huntington refuse to see *E. T.* and *Raiders of the Lost Ark* because Steven Spielberg has a complicated love life? What is this man talking about? What is he running for? Why is he vice president of the United States?

Mercifully, before the minds of citizens who had accidentally flicked onto C-SPAN and then remained there, paralyzed by boredom, could turn into complete porridge, the tube produced an infinitely more informative discussion of the dark side of American culture. Tipper Gore and Bill Buckley appeared, along with a rock critic from *The Village Voice*, to kick around the exploitation of sex and violence for profit by the entertainment industry. Since Tipper Gore, unlike Dan Quayle, has actually done something useful about all this — she being one of the chief instigators of the ratings system now used by the music industry — it was a pleasure to hear her educate Buckley on the subject. She combines respect for the First Amendment, appreciation of rock music, and a determination to protect children with modesty and common sense. After hearing Quayle, it was such a relief to listen to someone who knows what she's talking about.

Being a First Amendment feminist is not one of our society's easier roles these days. We often seem to be swimming through such a miasma of sexual violence — in advertising, television programming, heavy metal, rap, films, and worst of all, in the home — that even First Amendment absolutists sometimes daydream about how nice it would be to have government-as-nanny just outlaw all this effluent.

It is quite reasonable to subscribe both to the old saw that no good girl was ever ruined by a book and to the perception that it is not good for children to be constantly exposed to the sexual violence in our popular culture. Protecting children seems to me logically, legally, and rather easily differentiated from censorship — and good on Mrs. Gore for helping parents protect their children.

Sexism is comparable to racism in many ways, and one of them is that as racism has become less acceptable in our society, so have racist literature, films, music, et cetera. We have not outlawed racist expression, it continues to exist, you can order it from crummy mail-order houses in California. But you can no longer trot down to the Jiffy Mart and buy overtly racist magazines — not because of censorship, not because of laws, but simply because it is socially unacceptable. So eventually, pray God, will sexist literature and films be socially unacceptable. But anyone who thinks we can rid ourselves of pornography by passing laws against it needs to read more history.

The wonderful thing about the First Amendment is that while it protects even the most vicious and hateful forms of speech, it also protects our rights to condemn such speech — in terms just as powerful and as vigorous as we can manage. So that if I want to condemn peddlers of sexual violence for puking the rancid remainders of their sick minds all over this society, I am free to do so.

Fort Worth Star-Telegram, September 8, 1992

WITH U.S. MEDIA, MALICE IS ABSENT — BUT SO IS ATTENTION

Having recently been involved in media criticism in three different forums — including that ghastly soporific yawner of a *Nightline* special edition the other night — the topic is much on my mind.

Election season always brings out people who are mad because their candidate doesn't get written about or seen on TV the way they think he should. And the postelection season always brings a merry round of journalism conferences in which we slap our foreheads and beat our breasts and promise that next time we'll do it better.

The thing that surprises me most is that both journalists and our readers sit around criticizing what we do. The problem is not what we do. It's what we don't do. I think most journalists will go to professional hell (which is something like being edited by *The New York Times* copy desk for eternity) for their sins of omission, not their sins of commission.

The 1980s was a particularly grim decade for

journalistic dereliction of duty.

While we were busy keeping you informed about Bush's dislike of broccoli and about Donald and Ivana's love life, the whole S&L crisis — estimated cost upward of $500 billion — occurred without a peep from your watchdogs in the press. Had it not been for a newspaper in Beirut, we would have missed the Iran-*contra* scandal entirely.

Washington, D.C., which boasts more journalists per square inch than anywhere else on earth, hadn't even the wit to spot the open scandals at HUD, the EPA, and elsewhere in the federal bureaucracy.

And above all, despite the fact that David Stockman laid it all out for the press early in the Reagan administration, we never reported that the government was in the process of committing economic suicide with an untested and patently silly policy. Instead, we were bringing you "celebrity journalism," breathless accounts of what Calvin Trillin once listed as "glitzhounds, Eurotrash, dress designers and countesses from New Jersey."

It was the decade when *Vanity Fair* was the "hot book" among the magazines and political people liked to read *The New Republic* because it was so "unpredictable."

While reporters were missing major stories all around them, the pundit corps was increasingly peopled by those straight from the front lines of partisan political warfare. Kenneth Adelman, Richard Perle, Mona Charen, David Gergen, Caspar Weinberger, Edwin Meese, Patrick Buchanan, Jeane Kirkpatrick, and Henry Kissinger (briefly) were all Reagan-administration officials who became syndicated columnists.

Since columnists are supposed to have opinions — as opposed to reporters, who are supposed to have prefrontal lobotomies — you may see no great harm in this development. But I submit to you that training and experience as a reporter, while it doesn't always make a good columnist (look at Evans and Novak), does inspire some respect for the squiggly nature of truth.

To instill respect for the craft of journalism, there's nothing like going out to interview both drivers and all five eyewitnesses to an auto accident, and then coming back and trying to write an accurate story about what happened.

The great exception to this rule was Walter Lippmann, who never worked as a reporter but was the towering pundit of Washington.

OK, so Lippmann never covered a beat, but he brought to the trade a degree of learning unmatched since. There may be a few other exceptions. William Safire of *The Times*, a former ad man and Nixon speech writer, is not only a terrific writer but also a whale of a reporter. I can't imagine where he learned it.

The stories the press is most apt to miss are what Gene Roberts, former editor of *The Philadelphia Inquirer*, used to call "the stories that seep and creep." The ones no one ever calls a press conference to announce.

The classic example is the greatest internal migration in the history of this country: the mass migration of rural Southern blacks to Northern cities starting in the 1920s. The trend was never covered by the white press in this country.

Now that the eighties are over, we look up to find 37 1/2 million poor people among us; to find that the average American family hasn't been able to get by on one salary since 1973; that most of us are working longer hours and doing less well than we were a decade ago. How come you didn't learn that before 1992? Perhaps it is because no one called a press conference.

One of the stories the press doesn't cover well is the press. When Ben Bagdikian first published *Media Monopoly* in 1982, he found that fifty corporations controlled almost every major media outlet in this country: daily newspapers, magazines, radio stations, television stations, book publishers, and movie studios. By the time the revised edition came out in 1987, the number was twenty-nine corporations, and it is lower today.

At the end of World War II, 80 percent of American newspapers were independently owned. Today, almost without exception, they are owned by one of fifteen chains.

Hodding Carter, a sometime media critic, suggests that the Achilles' heel of most journalists is that we seek the approval of our peers. Having recently survived a small spate of approval myself (like getting invited on *Nightline*), I'm taking as my credo an observation once made by the great political organizer Saul Alinsky, who once got an award from some prestigious foundation.

He called his staff together and said, "Don't worry, boys, we'll weather this storm of approval and come out as hated as ever."

Fort Worth Star-Telegram, September 20, 1992

PEROT'S TEETERING MAY GIVE CANDIDATES AN ECONOMIC FOCUS

So here we are again, waiting for Perot. This time it seems more, well, silly than anything else.

No one believes the jug-eared billionaire with the attractive gift for sensible-sounding metaphors and the terminal case of self-righteous ego is going to be our savior this year or any other. But, ever optimistic to the point of idiocy, I'm in hopes that Perot will actually force Bush and Clinton to talk more realistically about the economy.

Let me be a little more realistic than that. It's possible Perot can make Clinton focus more realistically on the deficit.

Clinton's deficit plan is full of fudge factor. Not only is he counting on a peppy rate of economic growth — the end of this recession we've all been waiting to end for four years now — to close the deficit, he's also factored in a hefty chunk of that old Reagan standby, "waste, fraud, and abuse."

Remember how Reagan was always going to ferret out "waste, fraud, and abuse" in government, and by so doing, save us zillions of dollars? Well, Clinton is planning to "streamline management" and other neo-sounding buzzwords that supposedly will have the same magical effect.

To be sure, we'd all be terminally grateful if someone could cure the Pentagon of ordering seven-hundred-dollar hammers, but somehow, those zillions of dollars of savings just never seem to appear.

As for George Bush, I'm afraid it's a no-hoper. He's fallen off the edge of the earth. He's just gone as far as getting real is concerned. He's just gone totally negative on Clinton.

As we keep pointing out, he has no other option. He can't run on his record. He can't run as the candidate of change, and he has no ideas. Bush has become Mr. Bent Numbers. They're coming so fast and so phony the press can't even keep up. Undeterred by the complete absurdity of the 128-new taxes gig, Bush is still using that howler along with a new, and equally specious, charge that Clinton's economic plan "would cause 2.6 million jobs to be lost."

When you go into the numbers behind that (Michael Kinsley and others have valiantly waded into the mire), it's just so goofy it's unbearable. Just as an example, Bush charges that Clinton's support of new forty-miles-per-gallon fuel economy standards, to be phased in over ten years, would "cost 300,000 jobs."

In the first place, the Motor Vehicle Manufacturing Association, which is fighting the new fuel-efficiency standards just as fiercely as it did the last ones (which it now brags about, of course), actually claims the forty-miles-per-gallon standard could cost "between 150,000 and 300,000 jobs."

They arrive at that figure by assuming that anyone now working in any way at making cars that get less than forty mpg will be unemployed in ten years. In other words, that there will be no customers for cars that get forty mpg.

Bush's campaign will, of course, have the desired effect of driving up Clinton's negatives, so that even if Clinton does win, we'll all feel sour and depressed and be thinking, "Good Lord, is Clinton really the best this country can do?"

Look, I don't think Clinton is any Thomas Jefferson myself. But it is galling to see Bush take Clinton's perfectly decent record as governor of Arkansas — not terrific, you understand, not wondrous, not the greatest thing since Jackie Gleason, but quite a decent record — and twist it with those phony statistics.

The numbers he's using about Arkansas are so deceptive, you are left asking the obvious question, aren't you. So why'd the people in Arkansas reelect the guy five times?

But Bush isn't relying on phony numbers alone. He's out calling Clinton a "socialist," and said Sunday, "Governor Clinton is already talking about pulling together the best and the brightest — all the lobbyists, economists, lawyers — all those guys, liberal guys that were hanging out with him in Oxford when some of you were over there fighting, and have them solve America's problems."

I like that, the prep-school Yalie insulting Rhodes Scholars, who have heretofore been known mostly for becoming pompous members of the Establishment.

If Bush isn't attacking Al Gore for being an environmental extremist, he's attacking Clinton for being an environmental menace, pretending he can barely bring himself to say "fecal coliform bacteria," it's such a horrid thought.

Mr. Bush may not be aware of it, but those of us who live in the real world have heard "fecal coliform bacteria" plenty of times. Reminds me of the time Bush went to that grocers convention and thought the bar code was some wondrous new discovery. Too many years, too many limousines.

The conventional wisdom, which has been wrong all year long, now says this race is almost over. The end can't come too soon. In Monday's paper we read, U.S. SET TO OPEN NATIONAL FORESTS FOR STRIP MINING. Day after tomorrow, Bush, having vetoed Congress's repeal of the regulation that prohibits abortion counseling at four thousand federally funded clinics that serve poor people, will begin enforcing the ban. Since the administration has already gutted both sex-education and family-planning programs, we can look forward to a lot more unwed, teenage mothers — and to hearing Dan Quayle blame Murphy Brown for same.

Fort Worth Star-Telegram, September 29, 1992

213

THE REAL PEOPLE AND THEIR REAL ISSUES ARE REALLY THE BEST

My new hero is the guy with the ponytail from Richmond, Virginia, who stood up and said, "Could we focus on the issues and not the personalities and the mud? Could you, like, cross your hearts?"

He did what no one else in the country, not any of the media sharpies, has been able to do all year. He made 'em stick to the issues. Good on you, and your ponytail, sir.

But we still haven't got the right format.

Just having them stand there and say, "This is my plan," "And this is my plan," "And this is *my* plan" doesn't move us forward that much. What we need is some way to get them to say, "This is why your plan won't work" or "This is why my plan will work better."

We still need more than "Donahue Does Debate."

But on the whole, the Real People are doing better than either the media or the spinners, at both questions and instant analysis. *Mac-Neil/Lehrer* has a terrific panel of Real People who react right after the debates. No bores. No show-offs. No campaign-workers-in-disguise, which is what we keep hearing on the call-in shows.

C-SPAN is doing its usual yeoperson's work by bringing us the professional spinners, who, one must admit, sound increasingly silly.

I have always preferred Bush in his kinder-gentler mode, but the one question Bush really bobbled Thursday night brought out his fundamental problem this year. It was from a black woman who asked the candidates what the country's economic problems meant to them.

The bobble was initially understandable, since the woman misspoke, saying "deficit" when she meant "recession."

But she went on to talk about what it was like to lose a job, not be able to make a mortgage payment or a car payment. Moderator Carol Simpson also rephrased the question, but Bush still couldn't handle it. To use one of the year's most dreadful clichés, he just doesn't get it.

It reminded one of yet another dreadful cliché, the Defining Moment for Bush (for some reason, the media have gotten big on Defining Moments this year): Remember the Grocery Association Convention that Bush attended where he was so amazed and impressed by the bar-code scanner? The White House later put out a spin-control assault on that story, saying of course the president had seen a bar-code scanner before, he was just being polite.

But I've talked to the reporters who were there that day, and they all believe he'd never seen one before. Well, of course he hasn't. He's been in the White House for twelve years, not in the grocery stores.

And there it is. Too many years, too many limousines.

The thinness of Perot's Snappy Patter showed through this time. An act like that needs Funny Songs to go with the Snappy Patter.

Clinton occasionally verged on the slick and even the smarmy, but what we saw Thursday was an abbreviated version of the essential Clinton. He's got himself down to making only three policy points about any given issue. He used to reel off up to twelve in a row because he really cares about the stuff.

They can start measuring the drapes now. The Democrats are going to Washington.

This one's over.

Fort Worth Star-Telegram, October 20, 1992

BUSH'S LOOKING GLASS REFLECTS CHARACTER ISSUES OF HIS OWN

"There's no use trying," said Alice, "one can't *believe impossible things."*

"I daresay you haven't had much practice," said the Queen. "When I was your age I always did it for half an hour a day. Why, sometimes I've believed as many as six impossible things before breakfast."

— Alice's Adventures in Wonderland

Character, says George Bush, is the issue. George Bush. Says character is the issue.

Character, one supposes, comprises both principles and integrity. What are George Bush's principles, this man who accuses Bill Clinton of waffling? George Bush has been on both sides of the abortion question. He has been on both sides of civil rights. More recently, he has been on both sides of new taxes. He has been on both sides of Saddam Hussein. He says he is for a balanced-budget amendment while the deficit has increased

217

to $288 billion and he has asked for more money than Congress has actually appropriated. He has been on both sides of "voodoo economics."

In 1964, George Bush campaigned against Ralph Yarborough as a staunch opponent of the 1964 Civil Rights Act, the first great piece of civil rights legislation, which gave blacks the right to eat in the same restaurants and drink out of the same water fountains as whites. He was wrong, he was mistaken, and he has never admitted it. Why doesn't he admit it? George Wallace has.

As a Republican, despite his heritage from both his mother and his father as a moderate Republican, he first became active in the Goldwater wing of the party. Later, he became a moderate. Then he became a Reaganite. Then he became whatever he has been for the past four years.

Those who were around during Watergate may recall Bush's inane, burbling denial of the entire stinking mess. Those who recall his vice-presidential years may recall why *The Washington Post* described Bush in a 1984 editorial as "the Cliff Barnes of American politics — blustering, opportunistic, craven, and hopelessly ineffective all at once."

You may recall why George Will described him in those years as the "yapping lapdog of the Reagan administration."

George Bush and principle. There is one single issue on which George Bush has been resolute through the years, despite its unpopularity and defeat — a capital-gains tax cut that would disproportionately benefit the wealthy.

George Bush and integrity. You may recall when he said on national television that Walter Mondale has said our marines in Lebanon "died in shame." Mondale said they died in vain. Then he tried to prove with a dictionary that Mondale *meant* "in shame."

Texans may recall that in the early 1980s Bush tried to avoid capital-gains taxes on the sale of his Houston home by claiming that his real residence was Kennebunkport, Maine. The IRS wouldn't let him. Since then, he has claimed a Houston hotel suite as his home.

You may recall his 1988 campaign — a vapid, racist exercise, featuring the flag and Willie Horton, conducted while he carefully concealed the extent of the S&L fiasco and lied about his involvement in the Iran-*contra* scandal. In this campaign he has descended into rank McCarthyism with his unfounded charge that there was some impropriety about Clinton's having visited Moscow during a tour of European capitals and with his demogoguery implying that it was unpatriotic to oppose the war in Vietnam.

One reason Bush won in 1988 was his famous interview with Dan Rather about Iran-*contra*. Bush blustered, he fulminated, he attacked Rather. But he never answered the questions. And the reason becomes more apparent every day.

He was not "out of the loop." From George Shultz's memo to Tuesday's revelation of the John Poindexter cable that lists Bush among those supporting secrecy and concealment of the entire operation. A month after that cable was written, Bush made a speech saying, "Let the chips fall where they may. We want the truth. The president wants it. I want it. And the American people have a right to it. If the truth hurts, so be it. We've got to take our lumps and move ahead."

But he went right on with the cover-up and is still lying about it today.

His entire administration is embroiled in a massive cover-up of Iraqgate, the illegal use of American grain credits by Saddam Hussein to buy weapons. To cover up this piece of folly, the administration had to interfere in and then botch the prosecution for the largest bank fraud in the history of this country. The CIA, the FBI, and the Justice Department are now engaged in investigating one another in the farcical fallout.

It would be more farcical if Americans hadn't died fighting Iraq.

In every campaign speech he gives, George Bush is guilty of massive hypocrisy. In every campaign speech he gives, he twists his opponent's words (as he does on Clinton's stand on the Persian Gulf war), he twists his opponent's stands, and he twists his opponent's record. He is guilty of hypocrisy about the Clean Air Act, the civil rights legislation he was finally forced to sign, the tax bill he agreed to ("Congress twisted my arm," he whines).

Sure, George Bush is a decent individual. He's polite, he's loyal, he's kind to his children, and he has that endearingly goofy streak (did you catch his reference to "ninety-ninety hindsight" the other night?). But in his public life, George Bush has been anything but an exemplar of principle and integrity. When has George Bush stood for anything in his public life except the protection and advance of George Bush?

To suggest otherwise is a sick, sad joke.

Fort Worth Star-Telegram, October 22, 1992

ROSS MAKING LONG, BIZARRE DESCENT INTO "PEROT-NOIA"

Seldom can we give our president credit for finding the mot juste, but the word *nutty* does come to mind after seeing Ross Perot's performance on *60 Minutes*, doesn't it?

Perot's bizarre tale about how Republican dirty tricksters were going to unleash a doctored photo of his daughter Carolyn and disrupt her wedding gives some satisfaction to those of us who have been warning for months now that Perot is paranoid and much given to conspiracy theories. Told you so. In true conspiracy-nut fashion, Perot has decided that anyone who doesn't believe his conspiracy theory is *part of the conspiracy*. Does the FBI fail to find a scintilla of evidence to back up Perot's claims? Why, then, the FBI is clearly a tool of the dirty Republicans. Do the police say that Perot's source on this ridiculous alleged plot is a well-known fantasist? Why, then, the police must be in on it too!

Actually, "whacko" is not far off the mark for Perot either. In the first place, no self-respecting

222

political trickster would ever plan something like interrupting the wedding of an opponent's daughter. Why in hell would you want to create sympathy for your opponent? Any fool can see it would do nothing but help the opponent.

As I have pointed out before, being slightly paranoid is like being slightly pregnant: It does tend to get worse. What does it say about Ross Perot's judgment that he would choose to believe the unsupported word of this Scott Barnes person, who has regularly come up with dingbat scenarios? Perot's old, morbid preoccupation with wiretapping and the security of his family is, I suspect, being exploited by a clever con man. Be interesting to know how much Perot has paid Barnes over the years for "tips" on alleged plots to bug him and other farfetched schemes.

Perot's claim during the third debate that he had been the target of assassination plots was in the same vein. The idiotic claim that the Vietnamese had hired the Black Panthers to do him in (here's a guy who knows nothing about either the Vietnamese or the Black Panthers) is sheer crackpottery. Perot not only hired private security guards to augment the elaborate electronic security at his Dallas home, but according to one of the ex-guards, he used to patrol the lawn himself, rifle in hand. Now there's a happy thought for his neighbors in north Dallas. Perot also claims five Black Panthers once infiltrated the joint and went running across the lawn, from which the family dog chased them.

As the Dallas cop in charge of intelligence said: "Read my lips. It never happened." (In a wonderfully Dallasian footnote, the cop noted that there were only ever seven Black Panthers in all of Dallas, and two of them were informants for DPD, so the cops knew their daily schedule, which anyone familiar with Dallas will find entirely believable.)

Even before Perot's paranoia broke into public view in this astonishing fashion, the man was reinforcing the "Perot's-just-on-an-ego-trip" charge. His first political advertisements ("And the engine needs a Major Overhaul") were actually wonderful exercises in what's wrong and how we might fix it. But suddenly how we might fix it has disappeared from the Perot ads entirely, and instead we get these paid paeans of praise for Perot that would make Napoleon blush. Not a word about how to fix the economy, just the guy who takes care of Perot's boats on Lake Texoma telling us what a great man he is. Not to mention the unbiased opinions of his wife and children. Sheesh! To think Perot once offered the appeal of plain common sense. The guy thinks he's the reincarnation of Alexander the Great.

In a delightful development for the much-bashed media, George Bush suddenly about-faces and announces he's counting on the great American press corps, that fearless watchdog of democracy, to expose Perot's claims for the paranoid fantasies they are. Ah, every dog has his day. How the worm turns. Add your own cliché.

And we were afraid the tail end of this campaign might get boring. Ha!

Perot will clearly believe anything that sounds goofy enough — turns out that he bought into Danny Sheehan's Christic Institute fantasies. For those of you not au courant with Conspiracy Nut City, Sheehan is living proof that not all conspiracy nuts are on the right: Sheehan is the leading left-wing conspiracy guru of our time, having taken an actual tragic incident in Nicaragua and embroidered it into an all-purpose conspiracy called The Enterprise, in which the Pentagon, the CIA, and everybody else is involved in a vast, worldwide drug-running operation. Any day now, Sheehan is going to decide the pope offed Grace Kelly (no one ever dies by accident in Conspiracy City). Perot met with Sheehan several times and even flew him to Dallas. Great, with advisers like this, President Perot will make the late H. L. Hunt look sane in no time, thus accomplishing the difficult feat of rehabilitating the reputation of the man we had heretofore assumed to be the weirdest right-wing billionaire Dallas ever produced.

Fort Worth Star-Telegram, October 28, 1992

NO MATTER WHO WINS, THIS SLEAZY CAMPAIGN IS STRICTLY A LOSER

It's down and dirty now.

There's George Bush flailing his arms and declaring, "Ozone Man, Ozone. He's crazy, way out, far out, man." Great, George Bush the hipster president.

I'm not sure calling anyone as relentlessly sober as Al Gore "crazy" is going to cut it: When Gore had a moment of pep last week, it attracted national notice.

The television ads are bad enough, but wait till you hear the radio ads. Good Lord, have mercy on the poor old truth. And if you think the radio ads are bad, wait till you see the smear sheets being spread about Bill Clinton in East Texas. "Baby killer" is about the nicest thing they're calling him on the charming bulletin being spread by Tyler Republicans.

When you need a reality check, you might remind yourself that if Clinton's record as governor of Arkansas remotely resembled what the Bush ads claim, it ain't likely the people would have reelected him five times. Unless, of course, you agree with Bush that Arkansans are "the lowest of the low." Also, as a matter of public record, Clinton has never proposed a "carbon tax," so it's unlikely this nonexistent energy tax will drive up your utility bills and cost jobs.

As of Friday, Clinton was two points behind Bush in Texas, and the Clinton campaign had pretty much decided to pull out and concentrate on the must-win states in the Midwest, which means there will be no Clinton response to the dirty radio ads that started here this weekend. There's an interesting story behind the National Rifle Association's nasty ads: Clinton got crossways with a big-deal lobbyist for the NRA a year ago. This hotshot out of Washington had Arkansas on his checklist for some silly bill to take away local rights to pass gun-control laws. As I heard the story, Clinton vetoed the thing not as a gun-control matter, but as a local-rights question, and the NRA lobster threatened right then and there to "get Clinton" in East Texas when he ran for president. Which is why we'll be hearing about how Clinton is going to take away our guns.

There's one promise George Bush has kept in this race: He said he'd do whatever it took to get reelected, and he has. How anyone going around telling people just flat-out lies can talk about character and trust is beyond me.

Not that the Democrats are blameless. If there's one kind of dirty campaigning that drives me crazier than others, it's attempts to scare senior citizens about Social Security. I just think scaring and worrying old folks for political advantage is unconscionable, and the Democrats are trying to do it in some ads. Sure it's true that Bush proposed across-the-board cuts, but he also specifically exempted Social Security. For the record, the only candidate who has proposed touching Social Security in any way is Ross Perot, who wants to make a higher proportion of the payments going to relatively well-to-do seniors taxable.

Meanwhile, the committed Perot-nistas don't seem overly troubled by the fact that their man sat there on national television last weekend with springs coming out of his head. It's one thing to dismiss almost everything you hear in the last week of a campaign as just politics — generally a sound practice in my opinion. It's another thing to overlook overt nuttiness on the part of your candidate.

I don't know about y'all, but this campaign is starting to get to me. As soon as I wake up in the morning, I hear myself saying: "Step one! Brush your world-class teeth. It's just that simple!" Then I stagger to the bathroom, peer at myself in the mirror, and say: "Who am I? What am I doing here?" While brushing my hair, I meditate gently: "What this country needs is more unity and compassion. We haven't got a person to waste. We need change. We can do better. Maybe if I change my part, I will do better." Then I hit myself in the head with a hammer a couple of times in honor of George Bush, and I'm ready for the day.

A weird machismo overcomes political people at this point in a campaign: They work themselves to a frazzle, and the press, everybody's favorite target this year, gets just as exhausted as the candidates. The watchdog of democracy is pooped, and the lies are flying thicker and faster than we can keep up with. Even Clinton, who is known for having the stamina of a horse, is dead on his feet by the end of a day now. Is this any way to pick a president?

Fort Worth Star-Telegram, November 1, 1992

NINETY-NINETY HINDSIGHT SAYS BUSH'S HUMOR WILL BE SORELY MISSED

I can think of one and a half reasons to vote for George Bush. The first is entirely selfish. But then, they tell us this is the year of the "What's-in-it-for-me?" voter.

What's in it for me as a political humorist is that George Bush is just fabulous material.

Bushspeak, the thing thing, that gloriously daffy streak he has — "Read my lips," "ninety/ninety hindsight," "the manhood thing."

Lord, but I would miss that goofy, preppy, golden-retriever-like part of his personality, those moments of transcendent dorkiness when we all stand there trying to believe he's just said what he did.

If you have any mercy in your hearts for those who make a living being funny about politics, take pity on us. Mark Russell is going to commit suicide if we elect Bill Clinton. *Saturday Night Live* will fall on its collective sword. Russell Baker will molt and decline. Mike Royko will be stuck with Chicago, and I'll be stuck with Texas.

Not that Texas isn't more than enough, but Bush has been such a boon.

The half-reason is foreign policy, and for none of the usual reasons cited by either Bush or the conventional wisdom.

I don't think Bush had do-squat to do with ending the cold war. Forty-four years of bipartisan American foreign policy and its own internal weakness killed off the Soviet Union. If any one person deserves a lot more credit than anyone else, well, they gave the Nobel Peace Prize to Mikhail Gorbachev for a reason. He was the one who put his life on the line. Likewise, it seems to me that Bush's leadership during the Persian Gulf war is canceled out by his stupidity in having armed Saddam Hussein in the first place.

However, I do think Bush deserves credit in an area in which he hardly ever gets it, and that's south of our border.

I grant you that saying his policies in Central America are better than those of Reagan is damning with the faintest praise in all of human history. And I'm willing to grant that NAFTA, as now negotiated, may well result in the faint sucking sound of jobs going south. But I still say that Bush — with his Hello-Jorge-this-is-George style of telephone diplomacy — has done better than any president since Kennedy (who mostly had plans rather than accomplishments) in improving our relations with Mexico and Latin America.

Except, of course, for Bush's ongoing drug-war

follies. There is immensely more the U.S. could do to help both our neighbors and ourselves south of the border, but the beginning, the minimum, has to be what Bush has accomplished. He has recognized the importance of the region, and given Latinos the respect they deserve and accorded them the dignity they must have.

And for the rest? Even if Bush has finally, belatedly developed some ideas, some weak domestic agenda, what makes anyone think he would have any better luck putting it into place next term than he has in this one?

Gridlock government will not only continue, it can only get worse with a bunch of sore-loser Democrats dominating Congress. As a lame duck, Bush will have even less clout. His judicial appointments won't get any better. The rot of cynicism and corruption that infected the second Reagan term will be back in spades.

And frankly, this Iraqgate mess is so rank, I'm afraid Bush will be impeached over it. Not the failed policy with Saddam Hussein — that was just a dumb mistake — but the cover-up. Like Watergate, the initial mistake was not as poisonous as the lies that followed.

The Bush administration has clearly jacked around with the prosecution of a criminal case, this immense BNL scandal out of Atlanta. And they're going to get nailed for it. The taxpayers have been nailed for a billion bucks. Just what we need: a second-term administration totally absorbed in an impeachment fight while the economy continues to unravel.

And if you really want to depress yourself, there's always the possibility that Bush will croak and leave us stuck with Quayle. Although personally, I have always thought God would never be that unkind.

As for the Perot option, damn, *damn!*, I wish with all my soul that had worked out. I would have loved that more than anything in the world. An antiestablishment populist with no strings on him, owning no one, not having to dance with a single special interest, just going up there to do the will of the people.

That is the dream of my life. We may never get this close again, and it is breaking my heart. I would have given my left arm for Ross Perot, and my right as well — except for one thing.

The guy's a wrong 'un. He is just not a democrat. The other night on television with David Frost, he kept saying, "I'm the only one who listens to the people." Bull. Perot listens to no one. Or more precisely, what he means when he says "the people" is the people who tell him, "Ross, we love you." Everyone else, he's exed out.

It's his way or nothing. That's why he quit the first time. He gutted his own corps of volunteers except for the ones who tell him exactly what he wants to hear. That squirrelly little part of his brain that will never allow him to admit he's wrong about anything comes up with these fantastic rationales for his own flaky behavior. A Perot presidency would be like the time of the papist plots in England. Conspirators sighted everywhere, evidence no object.

Look, I'm not a shrink. I can't tell you why he's like this. I just know from studying his record that Perot is not temperamentally suited to lead this country. He does not have the patience. He does not have the knowledge, and despite his seeming common sense, I don't think the man has the first idea how to go about getting anything done in D.C. Worse, he couldn't and wouldn't stand having anyone around him who did know.

George Bush once said the key thing we should watch, the one that would tell us more than anything else, was who he chose for vice president. Bush chose Dan Quayle. Perot chose Admiral Stockdale. Stockdale is admirable in many ways, but he is not a democrat, and he could no more function as president than he could put on a pink tutu and dance *Swan Lake.*

So that leaves Clinton. I reserve the right to make fun of Bill Clinton from now to infinity, but he is bright (actually, amazingly bright) and he has a sense of humor about the world and about himself. He genuinely likes people, even the ones who don't grovel at his feet, and he listens, which is an unusual trait in a politician.

He is a serious student of how you get government to work. In fact, that is the great passion of his life. More than that, I don't guarantee.

Clinton is gonna have to dance with the people what brung him, and I do not know if he has the political courage to change that system. So maybe

234

the best solution is to go out and vote for him and make sure he knows we *all* brung him.

Finally, to all my old friends, and to all my old enemies, concerning what I fear will always be the Defining Moment for our generation. I think the question now is not whether you went to Vietnam or whether you didn't, whether you fought in the war or whether you fought against the war. I think the only question is whether we can find a president smart enough never to make a mistake like that again.

Fort Worth Star-Telegram, November 3, 1992

EXPECTING CAMELOT WITH A TWANG? TRY MUDVILLE WITH A BRAIN

John Kennedy may have been young Bill Clinton's first political hero, but Bill Clinton is no John Kennedy. Kennedy was part of the American aristocracy — wealthy family, private schools, formal dances with white tie and tails. Bill Clinton is as common as either mud or Abe Lincoln, depending on how you want to look at it.

The way he got to Georgetown University, a Rhodes scholarship at Oxford, and Yale Law School was by making top grades at Hot Springs High School. And the people he knows, the people he comes from, and the people with whom he has spent most of his life have Southern accents, bad grammar, and callused hands.

A bunch of them have been having breakfast at the Waffle House in Jacksonville for the past couple of days, not as a political statement, but because they always have breakfast at the Waffle House. (Had George Bush ever had breakfast at a Waffle House before this campaign?)

They're split on Clinton, and a lot of them didn't vote. The guy with the plumbing-supply company would have, but he thought there was a law that they had to give you time off from work to vote, and it turns out there's not. By the time the waitress finished her shift, it was too late. Bud from Little Rock had to wait two hours to vote.

And none of that should have happened. Texas has pioneered on early voting, and I think the results are good enough so we should not only keep it and extend it, we should recommend it to the rest of the country. About a third of Texans voted early this year, in lines that moved right along and took maybe ten minutes. It's so much more convenient and easier, I figure we can get it down to where the only people who need to vote on Election Day are the procrastinators and the chronically undecided.

Of all the jiggering we need to do with the system — getting the polls to close at the same time or the networks to hold off on predictions, motor-voter registration, same-day registration, and so on — I believe Texas has come up with the best and most important innovation in years.

I thought Al Gore had the two best lines on election night: "Where I come from, they call that character" and "It is time for us to go." I thought George Bush's concession speech was Bush at his best. It was enough to make one grateful for WASP cultural training. WASPs may not be in touch with their emotions, but there's a lot to be said for a tradition that teaches that you never cry in public and you never whine when you lose. I heard some grumbling about the line on "honor" in the presidency, but I thought he did well.

A correction on the oft-heard charge that Clinton has never had anything but a government job. He spent three years teaching constitutional law, and I can't think of better training for the job he's about to start.

All in all, it's been a glorious election. From the day Clinton said he never inhaled to George Bush's debate with the guy in the chicken suit, it's been one thrill after another.

Fort Worth Star-Telegram, November 5, 1992

OILMAN'S NATURE ROOTED IN STANDARDS FEW COULD EVER LIVE BY

J.R. Parten of Madisonville died yesterday, leaving Texas shy of both the vision and the integrity that have enriched our state for many years.

Parten was a very old man when he died, ninety-six, I believe, still active and clear almost to the very end. Parten was one of the great independent oilmen of Texas, and in that field alone, his knowledge and wisdom were formidable. But he was also a great citizen. In fact, when he was a student at the University of Texas, he majored in both law and government because he felt that no matter what one did in life, one always had another responsibility as a citizen, and Parten wanted to be prepared for his.

President Roosevelt also named Major Parten (he served in World War I) to a commission that went to Europe right after V-E Day to inspect the damage and make recommendations on what the U.S. could do to help repair what was always referred to as "war-torn Europe." This later became the foundation for the Marshall Plan.

I always liked a story Parten would sometimes tell about a big-deal industrialist who was on that commission and who was incredibly rude and condescending to our then-allies, the Soviets. "I had to send him home," said Parten simply. "His manners were so bad." Parten, tall, blue-eyed, erect, the soul of integrity, was also a gentleman. Of course he was a capitalist and an oilman, but his admiration for the fight the Soviets put up against the Nazis never dimmed.

Parten served on the University of Texas System Board of Regents from 1935 to 1941, and was chairman for two years. His accomplishments included the hiring of Homer Rainey to head the Austin campus, and Dana X. Bible to be its football coach. The pinheads and know-nothings in the Legislature later fired Dr. Rainey, and Parten was in the thick of the battle to save him. I don't know that Parten was ever liberal in his views, but he was an immensely civilized man, with a deep reverence for the Constitution. He read widely and had great faith in this country. Of course, he himself had gone from picking cotton in East Texas as a boy to the university and on to become one of the wealthiest men in the country. So he always worked to make sure others had the same kind of opportunities.

His contempt for small-minded people who were afraid of any change or any new ideas was always gently expressed, but profound. During the McCarthy era, Parten was so troubled that the guarantees of his beloved Constitution were giving way before the waves of fear and hysteria that he set up the Fund for the Republic to help provide money for scholarship and to publish the work of those who felt the Constitution was more important than the Communist Menace.

Parten had a couple of big ranches near Madisonville where he bred cattle, and those places were one of his great loves. He used to say, "The finest fertilizer any soil can have is the footsteps of the owner on the land." One of his great friends was the late John Henry Faulk, the Texas folklorist and humorist. Hearing the two of them talk about history and politics and the University and the Constitution and the oil bidness was an education, perhaps the best I ever received.

Parten was such a striking Texas figure, so at variance with the stereotypical Big Rich Texas oilman, that *The New York Times* once wrote him up as "The Real J.R." There wasn't an ounce of snob to him, but he simply could not bear the meretricious, or cruelty in any form. I once asked him about H. L. Hunt, whom he had known well, and after giving a balanced and indeed rather charming account of that highly eccentric man, J.R. shook his head and said, "But I never could forgive him for the way he treated his oldest son — I never could."

I knew Parten only as this admirable part of Texas history: I think he was a great man, but I doubt he was an easy one to be close to. He had such extraordinarily high standards of conduct himself — such integrity, he was a man of such astonishing rectitude — that it was not easy for lesser mortals to be around him. I always thought part of Parten's life was rather sad — sad that such a gifted man of such exceptional character, who was so devoted to his country, was never given more scope to serve it. After Roosevelt died, we never had a president with the sense to use J.R., but to the best of my knowledge, Parten himself had no regrets. He never repined. I suppose he thought it was akin to self-pity, and of course that would never have been acceptable.

It seems to me most of us go through life more or less knowing what is right, but not often or even usually able to measure up to our own standards, to always be what we would like to be. I never knew anyone quite as good as J. R. Parten at simply Doing the Right Thing without ever counting the cost, simply because it never occurred to him to do anything else.

Rest in peace, Major Parten.

Fort Worth Star-Telegram, November 10, 1992

CUT! IN THIS SCENE, YOU CAN'T JUST SAY NO

Now that Superman's dead, we may never get a school-finance bill through the Lege. In the latest chapter of this endless saga, which by now rivals *The Perils of Pauline*, the House Republicans have decided to tie the finance bill to the railroad tracks again. Help! Help!

In a display of provincial self-interest unusual even by the standards of the Texas House, we find the R's voting no on every conceivable combination that would lead to a solution. Said one observer, "It's like redistricting, with money added."

Gib Lewis, who has seen some legislative imbroglios in his time, says this is the most stuck he's ever seen the House and that there may not be a politically possible solution.

There is, of course. It will come when the schools are shut down next summer, and the citizens get so mad they threaten not just to throw the bums out but, in best Texas style, to hang the dumb s.o.b.'s. Then, suddenly, magically, all will fall into place, and they will hasten to do exactly what they could do right now. Trying, isn't it?

Basically, there are two possible solutions to our school-finance mess: We can either take some from the rich districts and give it to the poor districts, or we can pass new statewide taxes to pay for the whole system equitably. The R's have now voted no on both options.

The current wrinkle in trying to get some version of a Robin Hood plan passed is that the R's insist they won't vote for the plan in principle until they see exactly how it affects the school districts in their own patch. But when shown how it affects the districts in their own patch, they vote no.

An old Bob Bullock ploy is now being played out. Bullock, that wily old trout, has always favored giving the R's enough rope to hang themselves with. He baited and challenged the R's to come up with a plan of their own — since they refuse to vote for anyone else's — and now the fools have done it.

Of course, their plan, the Ogden bill, is a disaster. It does away with weights for vocational-agriculture, programs for pregnant students, bilingual ed, and everything else you can think of. The sound you are about to hear is that of superintendents screaming all over the state. After this memorably awful alternative gets demolished, they can try again on "fair share."

But here we are again, trying to put yet another new patch on top of all the old patches. We could, of course, actually try to do something for education in the state: slash administrative costs, consolidate districts, take the property tax out of the deal, take football (yes, football), track, volleyball, and all that good stuff out of the tax-paid budget and let the moms and dads raise money for it with school fairs and ticket prices.

Yeah, we could do that. All it requires is vision and statesmanship, which means we're in big trouble.

There is something particularly dispiriting about watching this level of parochialism on an issue that goes directly to the hoariest of the often-invoked gods of the Legislature (well, after "a healthy bidness climate") and that is "for the sake of the schoolchildren of Texas." Should the schoolchildren of Texas ever have gotten the idea from legislative rhetoric that they actually matter around here, a good look at this session will disabuse them of that illusion. We're going for the option that favors the taxpayers over their children, and so far we can't even get that passed.

The sordid spectacle of the special-interest groups in the educational establishment in there scrapping for their own self-interest is almost as revolting as the legislators' provincialism. Superintendents, coaches, teachers, boards, everybody's in it for the turf. Whew. No wonder Bill Hobby just gave up on it all.

Two helpful lessons may yet emerge from this sorry session.

One is, when next you hear some fool yipping about "local control," deck him. That old shibboleth is so clearly being used to protect entrenched special interests with no more concern about education than Rin Tin Tin that it should be permanently sidelined as a legitimate concern. One senator with an education background says not one single school district has eliminated one single thing from administration since going back to House Bill 72, and that in fact it's gotten worse. He's probably right.

Numero Two-o, anyone who thinks all this is better postponed until the regular session is rowing with one oar in the water. Can't you just see all this being played out again in the midst of regular-session madness, with six thousand other special interests competing to get on the agenda and that June 1 deadline looming?

Lest all this lead you to despair of democracy, keep in mind that a majority of both houses of our very own much-despised Texas Legislature have already voted twice for reasonable solutions to this mess. The first got thrown out by the very court that mandated the change in the first place (leading to no small degree of exasperation with those worthies), and the second is this best-patch solution, the "fair-share" plan. We are now stuck on the requirement for a two-thirds vote for a constitutional amendment, but at least we have a majority of responsible legislators. And for this much, let us all be devoutly grateful.

Fort Worth Star-Telegram, November 23, 1992

THANK YOU, GEORGE, DAN, MARILYN . . .

Meditating on gratitude in a mellow Texas November is one of life's sweller pastimes.

The week the Democrats won the White House and TCU beat UT, it seemed to be raining blessings. As a soul-scarred Texas liberal, I superstitiously wished the rate would slow down. I can't take that much good news all at once.

Texas liberals are the camels of good news. We can cross entire deserts between oases.

However, once given cause to rejoice, we're really awfully good at it. Most liberals, ever sensitive and compassionate to the point of making you want to throw up, are horribly good sports when they win. Personally, I believe in gloating. It's not enough for me that the Republicans lost; I'd just as soon they all had flat tires on the way home from the polls.

My mama may have raised a mean child, but she raised no hypocrites. I loved seeing those sorry right-wingers bite the dust.

I know, it is my liberal duty to pour sympathy

on everyone from milk-shy Hottentots to the glandularly obese, but after twelve years of being governed by these mean-spirited fools, I'm saving my empathy for the homeless.

I take the most exquisite satisfaction in the yowls of bad sportsmanship coming from the Bushies. Did you ever in your life hear such a caterwauling? Ever hear so much sour, boorish moaning? I especially like the ones who threaten to move to Australia. I feel sure they're the same people who like to impugn the patriotism of Democrats.

They're greeting Bill Clinton with all the generosity of spirit I have come to expect of them. (Hell, she said virtuously, when Ronald Reagan was elected, I actually hoped he would balance the budget.)

Of course, no recitation of Thanksgiving Day gratitude on my part would be complete without acknowledging the Divine Comedy the R's have so long provided. From the day they declared ketchup a vegetable to the selection of Dan Quayle as vice president of the United States, they have graced our land with laughter.

From the day Ronald Reagan laid a wreath in memory of the SS to George Bush's tour of Auschwitz ("Boy, they were big on crematoriums, weren't they?" he piped), I owe these guys for material.

I'd like to thank Bush for his immortal observation of child-rearing: "I mean, a child that doesn't have a parent to read to that child or that doesn't see that when the child is hurting to have a parent and help out or neither parent there enough to pick the kid up and dust him off and send him back into the game at school or whatever; that kid has a disadvantage."

I'd like to thank Dan Quayle for this thought on the fiftieth state: "Hawaii has always been a very pivotal role in the Pacific. It is in the Pacific. It is part of the United States that is an island that is right here."

I'd also like to thank Governor Lowell Weicker of Connecticut for his hedged but game support of the First Amendment: "I've always been a big supporter of the constitutional right of the people to peaceably assemble and petition government for redress of grievances. It's just that I never envisioned it taking the form of thousands of people screaming, 'You asshole, you asshole,' at me."

I want to thank Admiral James Stockdale for summing up the sentiments of Every American during this election: "Who am I? What am I doing here?"

Special thanks for the single day on which George Bush told the voters of New Hampshire, "Don't cry for me, Argentina. Message: I care," while also telling folks what a big fan he is of the "Nitty Gritty Ditty Great Bird Band."

Thanks to Marilyn Quayle, who in the course of denying that her husband had had an affair with an attractive lobbyist, said, "Anyone who knows Dan Quayle knows he'd rather play golf."

Thanks to Dan Q. (he really did contribute a lot) for this classic observation to the United Negro

College Fund: "And you take the model that what a waste it is to lose one's mind, or not have a mind as being very wasteful. How true that."

And again to George Bush (how I shall miss him): "Well, it appears to be a double standard to some, but I — that's my position and it's — we don't have the time to philosophically discuss it here. But we're going to opt on the side of life. And this is — that is the — that really is the underlying part of this for me. You know, I mentioned — and with really from the heart — this concept of going across the river to this little church and watching one of our children — adopted kid — be baptized. And that made for me — it was very emotional for me. It helped me in reaching a very personal view of this question. And I don't know."

And finally, I am grateful to Bush for this personal favorite of mine, from a campaign rally in California, "We're delighted to be here, Barbara and I. There's a danger. You have President Reagan, Governor Deukmejian, and George Bush. Watch out. Overdose of charisma! That's not too good."

God bless us, every one. Happy turkey.

Fort Worth Star-Telegram, November 26, 1992

"EXTRA" USED TO MEAN "EXTRA," AS IN "DO IT ON YOUR OWN TIME"

While the Lege attempts to jack itself out of the quagmire of school finance, the rest of us might want to contemplate some additional reasons why Johnny and Janie can't read.

An interesting document in this department is the Texas Education Agency's list of organizational activities for which a child can receive up to ten excused absences a year. In addition to an assortment of more or less academic-sounding organizations, we also find thereon: the Alamo Arabian Horse Association, the Palace Figure Skating Club of Dallas, the Houston Dressage Society, the National Rifle Association, and the National Baton Twirling Association.

We find, in addition, the American Drill Team School, the American Gymnastics Association, the Elks' Hoop Shoot, Miss Drill Team U.S.A. International, the National Cutting Horse Association, the Texas Amateur Racquetball Association, Ski Club Dallas, the U.S. Fencing Association, United

States Soccer Association, and the Amateur Confederation of Roller Skating.

All splendid activities, to be sure. But ten days of school a year to roller-skate? Doesn't *extracurricular activities* means EXTRAcurricular?

As the Lege struggles to pass this half-a-loaf school-finance deal, we are reminded of more serious, underlying problems in state government. One is, we're wasting all this time and effort to pass a school-finance bill that does nothing to improve education, which is really unforgivable. If you're going to have a knock-down drag-out, at least make it about something more than balancing the inadequacies of the current system. At least, hold out for some real improvement.

I know. They tried, and the court knocked it down. They still should try again.

Numero Two-o, the reason we're in this pickle is because our politicians are once more lying to the people. All right, so it's not outright lying; it's more failing to level with the people, which is surely a form of lying. Seems to me much of our presidential election this year centered on the same problem. There was George Bush, saying, "What recession?" while the rest of us were losing our jobs. The simple failure to recognize what everybody knows is happening is what gets pols into trouble. And they do it because they assume people would rather hear sugarcoated fairy tales than grim reality. For at least the 2,976th time: People are not stupid.

People are willing to pay for good schools. An

astonishing number of Texans were under the impression that the money from the lottery would be dedicated to the schools (it goes into the general fund). And it is painfully obvious that the only way to pay for good schools is with a statewide tax. You could do it with a property tax, but an income tax is fairer.

Besides Garfield Thompson's biennial, quixotic attempt to win support for a state income tax, the only other pol I know willing to stand up and say that is Representative Paul Sadler, D-Henderson (though Bullock gets credit for having tried).

Which leads us to an ominous political problem: Where is the Democrats' bench strength in state politics these days? Where's the B team? Used to be you could think of a half-dozen or more Democrats you'd like to see in statewide office. Comptroller John Sharp is only the logical future governor. Mauro's damaged, Morales is in trouble, Lena's gone. And only Sadler has the courage to raise hell in the House.

Now here's an interesting bit of evidence of why political reporters should continue to follow the First Rule (Look at the record). Because when political people talk about the dearth of courage in the Legislature, all of them, Republicans and Democrats, liberals and conservatives, use the same example: "Where's the Johnny Bryant?"

Johnny B., now a U.S. representative from Dallas, raised hell in the Lege in the late seventies, challenging the Speaker with his less-than-mighty Gang of Four. And just to show you how true political bloodlines, and performance, run, here's Bryant in Congress, the only member of the Texas delegation recognized by the Financial Democracy Campaign for his "watchdog" record on the banks. (Phil Gramm scored a perfect zero.) That kind of courage shows early, so keep an eye on Sadler.

Because the Clinton campaign did not contest Texas, Democrats here had a particularly grim year. In addition, Texas Republicans, who used to elect the occasional Fred Agnich or Jack Vowell, have now started electing Pat Robertsonites. When Betty Andujar starts looking good in retrospect, you know new lows are being set.

If Texas Democrats want to have a party at all, I suggest they get their derrieres in gear and do something about it — now.

Fort Worth Star-Telegram, November 29, 1992

THIS PUNDIT'S SECRET

The biggest fool in America for over a year now has been the Conventional Wisdom, the collective judgment of Washington pundits, political insiders, wise men, Capitol cognoscenti, Beltway buffs, and other purveyors of inside skinny on where our collective political enterprise stands. They have been wrong — dead, flat, utterly wrong — at every turn.

I noticed this because I myself happen to have been right all year long by virtue of my old standby — that is, the reliable stopped-clock method. My record is the following: In 1968, I refused to believe the American people would actually vote for Richard Nixon; in 1972, thought George McGovern could break 40 percent; in 1980, considered Ronald Reagan a bad joke and in 1984 a worse one; and in 1988, dubbed George Bush too hopeless a twit even to win the Republican nomination. How wise these judgments seem now, when retrofitted.

By the same reliable methods of political divination, I announced last spring that anybody could beat Bush this year. That was the point at which no one would run against him. Lone and lorn stood I against the snickers of the crowd as all hailed the Hero of Desert Storm and counseled the Democrats not to bother running against him — roll over and play dead, this one's gone, they said.

That Bush's numbers had been lousy before Desert Storm and were rapidly returning thither seemed to impress no one but me. As late as last fall, when Bill Clinton announced his candidacy, the Say-Theyers thought it was all bootless. Nameless pygmies like Clinton and Tsongas, for pity's sake, to challenge the peerless prexy. None of the big guys wanted to play. Bradley of New Jersey, Gephardt of Missouri, Gore of Tennessee — all had assessed and judged it a no-hoper.

The pundits sat around waiting for Cuomo for months — all fall, through the holidays, and into the new year. In January, *Vanity Fair* thought Bob Kerrey was inevitable. In late February, *Newsweek* once more resurfaced the Cuomo Possibility. By March 3, "Junior Tuesday," the Democratic nomination had been decided, later contests to the contrary notwithstanding. A Democratic T-shirt of that era read, I AM — ALL THINGS CONSIDERED, AND CONSIDERING THE ALTERNATIVE — UNLESS HE DOES SOMETHING ELSE THAT REALLY PISSES ME OFF OR THERE TURNS OUT TO BE ANOTHER BOMBSHELL — FOR BILL CLINTON FOR PRESIDENT. Meantime, after my newspaper was shot out from under me, three months on the unemployment line convinced me that *malaise* did not begin to cover the mood of the voters.

I spent a month trying to get the pundit corps to take Ross Perot seriously, which they finally did, writing alarmed screeds announcing, The Voters Are Pissed! They're Really Pissed *This* Time! By then it was clear that Ross Perot knew no more about running for office than a hog does about Sunday, and was all hawk, no spit anyway.

WHY CLINTON CAN'T WIN, said the inviting headline on the cover of the May 4 *New Republic*. *Time* magazine pronounced Clinton dead on the "trust issue" at the same time. Two months later, both magazines were assuring us that Clinton couldn't lose.

Not everyone was wrong, of course. *Time*, using my stopped-clock method, predicted Al Gore would get the vice-presidential nod — back in 1988. *The New York Times* asked this prescient question: "Is America ready to elect a confessed adulterer as president?" And answered, "No," adding, even more presciently, "Not in 1988, anyway."

By early August, the pundit corps was busy working variations on the Bush-is-dead-meat theme. Numero Uno, they said, he should dump Dan Quayle (no reference here to January's Quayle boomlet, for example, *Newsweek*'s "A New Boost for Quayle — Respectful Articles"). Numero Two-o, Bush should dump himself. The president was in ill health, sick, tired, looked terrible, was going to drop out.

In mid-August, Bush announced that Jim Baker would quit as secretary of state to run the president's reelection campaign. Bush then enjoyed the greatest resurrection since Jesus'. Now we would all see miracles indeed; lo, the political wonders Baker would perform.

To the best of my knowledge, no seer but myself noticed the true turning point of the campaign. In supreme modesty, I point out that I alone held forth on the gladiator-biting-the-lion-in-the-balls story. This signal development in American political history occurred when Bush addressed a convention of conservative state legislators in Colorado Springs and told the following tale: In ancient Rome there was a great gladiator who killed every lion they could throw against him. The centurions were jealous of him, and they went to Thrace and got the worst, meanest lion there ever was. Then they buried the great gladiator in sand up to his neck in the middle of the arena and let the terrible lion loose. As the lion charged toward the gladiator, and as it made the first jump over his head, the gladiator bit the lion, in the most sensitive portion of his anatomy, and the lion howled and ran from the arena. The centurions rushed in and said to the great gladiator, "Fight fair, dammit, fight fair."

Right away, you fail to see the significance of this. So did the audience. So George Bush (the only president we've got) had to explain: "Every time I tiptoe into the water against this guy, they rush in saying, 'Negative campaigning, negative campaigning.' " A report in *The New York Times* on this speech said it had been put together by a scribbler hired to help George Bush "connect with the common man."

Here's the analysis: Getting ready to be renominated, Bush saw himself as the gladiator buried in sand in an unfair fight — the economy had been unfair to him, barfing on the prime minister of Japan had been unfair to him, the tear gas in Panama had been unfair to him — he was up to his neck. So all he could do was bite Bill Clinton in the "most sensitive portion of his anatomy." And it was so unfair for people to call it "negative campaigning."

Poor George. He's the only politician I can think of — in 1992, that is — who would strive to connect with the "common man" by telling a story about Roman gladiators and referring to the "most sensitive portion of his anatomy" when he meant biting Clinton in the balls. But stopped-clock analysis says: Mark your calendar. By 1996, there will be a whole bucketful of them, a new generation of wannabes — all hat and no cattle — buried in the sand, jaws slack, waiting for new opportunities.

Mother Jones, November/December 1992

REINDEER ARE COUNTED
BETTER THAN HOMELESS

Aunt Eula wrote from Fort Worth to inform me that in 1954, fifty thousand reindeer migrated from Lapland to Finland. An interesting seasonal note, but the most interesting thing about it is that we know it. Someone counts migrating reindeer so we know if they're up, down, or holding steady. Try getting an accurate count of the homeless in America. Or even in Fort Worth . . .

You can find an estimate for New York City — serendipitously enough, it is fifty thousand, the same as the migrating reindeer of '54. After that, we start wandering up the scale — 250,000 across the country, 1 million, multiples of 1 million. No one actually knows. Obviously, at least some students of this problem are off in their count by at least a million people.

Oh, no! — I hear your vast collective groan — not another Christmas Column on the Homeless! Well, you know how it is with us liberals, we just can't help ourselves; like Dr. Strangelove, our hands rise involuntarily, despite our best intentions, and write these Christmas Columns on the Homeless, thus managing to be boring and trite simultaneously, laying our liberal guilt all over an unwilling general populace. But grit your teeth and soldier on, if you will, in seasonal goodwill.

Not only do we not know how many Americans are homeless, we don't know much about those who are. The most common form of denial about homeless people is that they deserve to be where they are. They're drunks, winos, bums, addicts. Their condition is self-inflicted and thus not our fault. We have no responsibility. It's not my fault, I'm all right, Jack.

The concept of addiction as a treatable disease has not made that much progress, despite the best efforts of the Alcohol and Drug Abuse Council. Many of us still think these are the Undeserving Poor. (Wouldn't you think some sociologist would have done a comparative study by now to prove, as I have always suspected, that there is a higher proportion of Undeserving Rich than Undeserving Poor?)

But we know there is an additional admixture in our homeless population now, one there, as conservatives never tire of pointing out, because of one of those brave, new, liberal social experiments gone wrong.

Lots of nut cases are on the streets these days as a consequence of the movement in the sixties and seventies to deinstitutionalize people who are not dangerously insane. Since it was incredibly expensive as well as counterproductive to keep those folks incarcerated, it seemed like a good idea at the time to let them go home and get treatment there. And as liberals never tire of pointing out, the reason deinstitutionalization was such a failure is because the chintzy conservatives in the legislatures never appropriated enough money for community-based mental-health care.

As a result, we have nut cases on the streets getting no care, some of whom are quite dangerous because they get no care. For all our brave, new sophistication about mental illness, many of us still react to crazy people with primitive fear — don't get close, you might catch it.

Blame and fear. The trouble is, not only have blame and fear never built a single unit of low-cost housing, they don't cover the situation anymore.

All recent studies of homeless populations show an increase of two groups out on the streets — families and people with full-time jobs.

You may well ask why we should pay any attention to studies done by the same people who can't even get a firm count on how many people we're talking about, but the consistency of the results makes them hard to ignore.

About one-third of the homeless are now families, and about one-fourth work full-time for the minimum wage. Their problem is simple: They can't afford housing. So is the solution — build more low-cost housing.

Perhaps it is precisely because of the studies showing that the majority of American families are only a couple of paychecks away from the street

262

themselves that we resist thinking about this. That's how denial works: The closer we get to whatever frightens us, the more vigorously we deny that it will touch us.

In several localities, we have now reached the apogee of idiocy by trying to outlaw the homeless.

Some of our professional hand-holders of the middle-class have lately been worried about "compassion burn-out." What with the Somalis and the Bosnians and that assortment of other misbehaving foreigners, it is feared that the American public will wear itself to a frazzle worrying about others, resulting in a general concern shortage.

As I have yet to witness an overabundance of concern for our fellow citizens now freezing to death on the streets of America, compassion burn-out is not high on my list of priorities.

It is not often that we have a major public problem to which there is a simple solution. During the Reagan years, about $3 billion was cut from low-income housing programs, and homelessness, amazingly enough, grew apace. Three billion is peanuts in the context of the military budget. We know what to do, we know the solution is not particularly costly, and here we are, doing what?

"Hark!" the traditional beginning of the Christmas message of joy, is, according to my Aunt Eula, the start of a message that has gotten garbled in translation.

Fort Worth Star-Telegram, December 22, 1992

263

THE NEW WORLD DISORDER

The nice thing about the Transition Period is that it gives Democrats something to gossip about. Take the situation here in Texas, where Bill Clinton picked off our senior senator, Lloyd Bentsen, and then picked off his obvious replacement, Henry Cisneros, leaving the field wide open for two generations of Texas Democrats to have a destruction derby.

Our poor governor, Ann Richards, is faced with a list of suggested replacements ranging from Ladybird Johnson to Barbara Jordan to Willie Nelson. I'm rooting for Dolph Briscoe, a 1970s-era governor and the most boring one we've ever had. In fact, Briscoe was the pet rock of governors, and I think he would be right restful in office. Never bothers anyone with charisma or ideas. He was given to appointing dead people to various boards and commissions, and they, too, were restful, caused no trouble at all.

And what, you may ask, does the Bentsen appointment as secretary of the Treasury say about the incoming Clinton administration? In short, it says, "Forget about any serious proposals aimed

at creating more economic justice in this country."
If Bentsen has ever shaken a bush on behalf of
economic justice, I missed seeing it twitch. He's
pure Tory Democrat.

On the other hand, Henry Cisneros is seriously
New Breed. Perhaps you have to be a Texan to
appreciate the full range of cultural values implied
by "Chicano Aggie" — a Mexican-American graduate of Texas A&M University — but that's what
Cisneros is. In addition, he has the Lazarus factor;
people reach out to touch his robes. If you ever
get a chance to hear the next secretary of Housing
and Urban Development speak, race right down
to the site. On his bad days, he's mildly terrific;
on his good days, he's electrifying. The quality
of his thinking and the quality of his caring are
both striking. Plus, he's pretty damn good at getting things done at a time when politics has become
the fine art of finding that sliver of daylight in
the wall of obstruction that prevents anything from
getting done about anything.

I, as a professional antiestablishmentarian, am
in the peculiar pickle of actually knowing several
people in the Clinton Cabinet. So far, it feels really
rotten to have any claim at all as an insider. I'm
taking as my motto a statement Saul Alinsky once
made to his organizers: "Don't worry, boys, we'll
weather this storm of approval and come out on
the other side as hated as ever."

That said, I know Alice Rivlin, deputy-direc-
tor-to-be of the Office of Management and Budget,
as someone who is not only smart but wise. She's

265

also short, quiet, and shy, living proof that women don't need assertiveness training: There is a quality of intellectual excellence that doesn't need to thrust itself forward; everyone around just notices it.

My friend Donna Shalala, the next secretary of Health and Human Services, is, on the other hand, a pistol. She is one of the most energetic, enthusiastic, and disciplined people I've ever known. Challenged by a fellow journalist to find something negative to say about Shalala, I pointed to her obvious and obnoxious habit of knowing everybody who is anybody. She is so notorious for this among her friends (often referring to world-famous folks as "Fuzzy" or "Muffie" or some damn thing) that we all cherish the story of Shalala's childhood softball team. When she was growing up in Cleveland, at about the age of ten, she played on a girls' softball team. The coach was George Steinbrenner. True story.

As we all limp into the New World Disorder, I figure we should be delirious with excitement, glee, and optimism. After all, this may be as good as it gets for the next four years, so we might as well enjoy it while we can.

As Roy Blount observed, I still believe in Hope — mostly because there's no such place as Fingers Crossed, Arkansas.

The Progressive, February 1993

266

AND THE ASSAULT ON THE CONSTITUTION GOES ON

Exit, smelling.

President Bush's Christmas Eve pardon of the major figures involved in the Iran-*contra* scandal stinketh. It leaves us with the rancid odor of the worst of the Reagan/Bush years once more clogging our collective nostrils, and it is enough to gag a maggot. On a level more important than how it smells, it does real damage to the Constitution.

Please acquit me of partisan political vengeance: I was among those who thought Richard Nixon, whom I loathed as one of the few figures of real evil I ever saw in American politics, should have been pardoned. Both Reagan and Bush are, by comparison, merely amiable doofuses. But the Watergate pardon was justified because even though the letter of the law had not been satisfied, the larger purpose of the law had been — the whole story was known, punishment had been meted out (the man was driven from office in disgrace), and the *lesson* was clear to everyone: Thou shalt not break the law with impunity, no matter who the hell thou art.

Bush's rationale for the pardons is manifestly unacceptable: He claims those involved were motivated by "patriotism." No one ever questioned it. Of course, Caspar Weinberger is a patriot. The poor man also opposed the entire misbegotten folly of Iran-*contra* from the git-go, and that is precisely the kind of mitigating circumstance the law is designed to include in the accounting. That Oliver North thought he was doing the right thing is beyond doubt.

But by what insane logic is misguided "patriotism" an excuse for perverting the entire premise of a government of the people, by the people, and for the people? Iran-*contra* included literally the setting up of a secret government, the financing of a secret government, to carry out policies made in secret, without the advice, consent, or knowledge of the people or their elected representatives. It included a consistent policy of lying both to the people and to their representatives. In no way did those who set out on this folly seem to consider themselves accountable to anyone or anything except their own weird Boys' Adventure sense of how to conduct the affairs of a democracy. They felt no obligation to observe their oath to protect the Constitution, nor were they troubled by the several laws they broke with a sense of self-righteous superiority.

If there has been partisan bashing in all of this, much of it has certainly been aimed at special counsel Lawrence Walsh. True, his investigation has dragged on through years now, costing lots of money by all-but-Washington standards. But the length and expense of that investigation were caused by precisely the continuing cover-up Walsh has been investigating. Not until 1990 did Walsh finally get key evidence he needed, and not until December 1992 did he get some, not all, of Bush's own notes on the affair.

I realize the presumption of innocence is still with those who are accused, or could be accused, but in all but matters of legal proof, we can take this sucker as read. We pretty much know what happened and even know that the root of the rot was the late Bill Casey, who is beyond the jurisdiction of anyone but the Almighty. So why pursue it? Because the lesson has not been learned; indeed, the lesson that one can violate the Constitution with impunity was learned instead, with the consequence that some of the players did it again in the Iraqgate matter, conducting a secret policy in violation of the law and then using the Justice Department to help cover it up. A perversion of the very sense of the word *justice.*

So little impressed is this crew by the requirements of law that even now they use it to play their nasty, backstabbing games. Bill Safire of *The New York Times,* who has done a superb job on Iraqgate all year, reports that Attorney General William Barr, who is a disgrace to his position, said no to further investigation of Iran-*contra,* no to further investigation of Iraqgate, but yes to a special prosecutor in the relatively piddly matter of some folks at the State Department looking into Bill Clinton's passport file. The reason? Barr's mentor is White House Counsel C. Boyden Gray, who has a long-running feud with former secretary of state Jim Baker, and Gray wants to embarrass Baker. Gives you a lot of respect for the majesty of the law, doesn't it?

Do I think Bush or Weinberger or anyone else should be sent to the slammer over this? No. All I want is a mea culpa. Those who have been lying need to quit lying, say, "We did it, we were wrong, we have done harm to the country and to its essential ideals, and we are profoundly sorry." It may not sound like much in the way of a pound of flesh, but letting lies fester is dangerously unhealthy to the body politic.

On a frankly political level, those who have pooh-poohed the seriousness of all this to protect a sitting president may want to reconsider whether the lesson, and the lesson unlearned, is one they want to let stand for the incoming Clinton administration.

Fort Worth Star-Telegram, December 29, 1992

MADONNA AND OTHER ARTHURS

I am worried about Madonna. OK, actually I'm worried about Madonna and me. Because of this woman, I'm in danger of being consigned to premature Old Poophood.

On the subject of Madonna, I resemble the Senate Judiciary Committee — I just don't get it. I achieve positively Bushian levels of not getting it.

I went along fine for quite a while with Madonna, feeling vaguely fond of her on the slender grounds that I understand her Fashion Statement. Although a lifelong fashion dropout, I have absorbed enough by reading *Harper's Bazaar* while waiting at the dentist's to have grasped that the purpose of fashion is to make A Statement. (My own modest Statement, discerned by true cognoscenti, is, "Woman Who Wears Clothes So She Won't Be Naked.") And Madonna's Statement is as clear as a Hill Country spring. It is: "I'm a slut!" What's more, it seems to be made with a great deal of energy and good cheer. I rather liked it.

But then Madonna took up *la vie littéraire*, invading my turf as it were, and I felt constrained to develop an opinion of her literary talents. Without, of course, reading her book, since no sane person is going to fork out fifty-seven bucks for her oeuvre. Even if she does have a comprehensible Fashion Statement. Careful study of the publicity about Madonna's book left me with a strong desire to say to her, "Young woman, stop making an exhibition of yourself." Since Madonna makes a living by making an exhibition of herself, it seemed a singularly bootless impulse.

C. R. Ebersole of Houston, who happens to be my former Sunday-school teacher, passed along his opinion that Madonna has done more for dogs than anyone since Albert Payson Terhune. I did not inquire why my former Sunday-school teacher paid fifty-seven bucks for a book called *Sex*.

Thinking I might be of the wrong gender to appreciate Madonna, I called my friend Aregood in Philadelphia, whose taste in women is notoriously ecumenical. Aregood says you can tell you're out of touch with your fellow Americans when the reigning sex goddess is someone you wouldn't take home with you if she were the last woman left in the bar. He also says Sophia Loren is still his idea of a sex goddess.

I struggled with the concept of impending Old Poophood. I was, in my day, fairly with it, verging on hip. When I was in college, I carefully suppressed the fact that I knew all the words to every song Bob Wills ever wrote, and listened assiduously to Bird Parker and Yves Montand. Later, I was among the first on my block to discover Bob Dylan, Janice Joplin, and The Band. You see, we're talking no mean record on the Cutting-Edge Front.

I admit to recent slippage — both punk rock and rap slipped right by me. But with the large tolerance that comes from being a nonparent, I have been given to loftily assuring my offspring-impaired friends that every generation is entitled to some form of music that will drive anyone over twenty out of the room. I believe this is meet, just, and probably part of God's plan.

Several of my advisers on contemporary culture have tried to persuade me that Madonna's redeeming social value lies in her apparently premeditated pattern of pushing all known taboos to the limit and beyond, in order to force her fans to think seriously about their own choices. Her fans seem to consist largely of thirteen-year-old girls. I believe this is a reflection of how difficult it is to be a thirteen-year-old female in our society.

When I was thirteen, I yearned to be an arthur. As I understood it, arthurs got to live in New York or Paris and hang out in sophisticated places like the Algonquin or Harry's Bar with terribly witty people, all of them exchanging bon mots that would later be collected by literary historians. Sounded like a good deal to me.

Then I became an arthur. All that happened was my publisher sent me to a lot of radio stations in places like Garden City, Kansas. No bon mots occurred.

I dunno. You grow up, you finally get to be an arthur, and there you are with Madonna. What the hell would Albert Payson Terhune say?

The Progressive, January 1993

BUBBA'S BOY?

The media — those friends, those archvillains, those ceaseless twisters of truth — have already mischristened the embryonic Clinton administration. They're calling it "Camelot with a Southern accent."

Wrong. Arkansas, the state Bill Clinton loves and that loves him back, is a place with just no pretension at all. Even for Southerners, Arkansans are amazingly friendly and extend hospitality to all strangers with astonishing openness. You couldn't find a pretension in that state if you hunted from Jonesboro to El Dorado.

True, Arkansas has its wiggy side. When I was there over Election Day, the radio preachers were involved in an arcane theological dispute over whether talking in tongues is really inspired by the Holy Ghost, and one local candidate has gotten himself in deep doo-doo by telling the Rotary Club that incest is a family matter (in its way, an unimpeachable observation).

Now just because a body has lived all his life among horny-handed sons of the soil (and a couple of refreshingly unaffected chicken magnates) is no

275

reason to assume we have a populist on our hands.

But do you remember that crazy senior citizen during the New Hampshire primary who kept screaming at Clinton, "What about drugs?" When he finally went over to find out what her problem was (most pols avoid screamers), it turned out the poor thing literally could not afford both her medication and food. When she broke down crying, Clinton went down on his knees, took her in his arms, and kept saying, "I'm so sorry," while they both wept. Kennedy? Not in a million years.

The most unusual thing about Clinton as a pol is that he listens. Listens and remembers. If he does dance with them that brung him, not them that gave him big money, we *will* have a populist on our hands.

And what would a real populist president do? First, change the banking system in order to democratize capital. The trouble with capitalism as a system is that only those who have or can get capital can make it work for them, and that leaves out damn near all of us. We need a new banking system. We could use the government protections of banks — FDIC, et cetera — for a new system of community-based, community-development banks. We know Clinton took a busman's holiday to spend time studying the South Shore Bank in Chicago to find out how it worked.

The Federal Reserve system obviously doesn't work anymore — they keep lowering the federal discount rate, and all that happens is that the banks are making a fortune and the old folks' CDs are getting chewed up. We need a real investment program in small businesses and co-ops and worker-owned plants, and that will have to include not just the capital, but also market development and training assistance, especially management training.

Even without doing a single new thing in banking, Clinton could help enormously if he'd just stop some of the old stuff that goes on. According to the Financial Democracy Campaign, the S&L bailout program continues to function as a bottomless welfare program for politically well-connected corporate and commercial interests. Some of the biggest purchasers of bargain-basement real estate from the Resolution Trust Corporation are members of the Republican "Team 100" and big Wall Street players.

On top of that, the Bush administration has been deferring what is by now a tidal wave of trouble in big banks — a thousand banks with combined assets of $500 billion are on the FDIC's "problem list." A decade's worth of risky leveraged buyouts, commercial real estate, home equity, and credit-card lending has left the taxpayers guaranteeing a system so shaky that when new bank regulations went into effect in December, a "December surprise" seemed almost certain. In a piece of incredible folly, the FDIC voted in September to reverse a modest increase in the premiums banks pay to the FDIC's Bank Insurance Fund.

Another useful exercise would be to go back and look at the tax loopholes the famous investigative team of Barlett and Steele found in the 1980 "tax reforms." Just reverse every one of those special-interest, lobbyist-inspired exemptions, let all the corporations pay at the same rate, and right there you'll pick up enough revenue to start closing the deficit. Of course the R's will scream, "New taxes, new taxes," but a loophole is a loophole, and those corporations that missed out before will be happy to lobby for a level playing field.

Clinton comes in with a promise to see to the economy before anything else, but the practical reality is that he needs to push through campaign-finance reform first, just to free the political system from the special interests. Tim Wirth, whose title as of this writing is "Al Gore's best friend," understands that perfectly — that's why he quit the Senate.

Now what does all this policy-wonk stuff have to do with what Bubba wants? Bubba thinks we can fix the special interests simply by putting in term limits. Look, Bubba may be wrong, but he's not dumb. All the president needs to do is lay out the bigger scheme for him; hell, Clinton can even borrow the charts and pointer from Perot.

Mother Jones, January 1993

278

IF I COULD WRITE CLINTON'S BIG SPEECH . . .

To my embarrassment, I recently misunderstood an assignment from Another Publication. This is the occasional lot of writers: Either too many editors tell you all too much about what it is they want (and no two editors have ever wanted the same thing), or some editor forgets to tell you the central premise of the whole effort.

Called upon to write a five-hundred-word version of Clinton's inaugural address, I did so — in all seriousness. Alas the gig was to be funny. So now I have this perfectly good speech sitting around and nothing better to do with it than offer it to you. So herewith, what I'd really like to hear Bill Clinton say on Inauguration Day:

My friends and fellow citizens, let me begin by thanking you. I am profoundly grateful for your support and for the trust you have given me. The honor of serving you as president is the greatest honor I can imagine and the greatest I shall ever have. I promise you that with every fiber of my being and every ounce of energy I possess, I shall

279

do my best to be worthy of your trust.

In some ways, I believe the task before this administration is not glamorous nor inspiring: I believe we are here to make this government work better. It is not the fault of any particular person or party, but in many of our institutions a sort of flabbiness and drift have combined with the inertia and notorious inefficiency of all bureaucracies to create government that does not work well, and sometimes does not work at all, to address the real problems of the people of this country.

I know better management does not sound like a particularly noble or glorious goal. Improving, streamlining, reorganizing, setting priorities — these are the tasks of technicians and efficiency experts. The application of intelligence and hard work to these tasks may be commendable, but it is not the stuff of great dreams or of inspiration.

But the reason I believe these rather mundane tasks are now so critical is that our driving dream as a nation is at risk if we cannot make it work better than this. We Americans are the heirs to the most magnificent political legacy any people has ever received. There are no new words better than the old words used to define that legacy at the beginning:

> We hold these truths to be self-evident, that all men — and women — are created equal, that they are endowed by their creator with certain unalienable rights, that among these are life, liberty and the pursuit of happiness.

We believe that to secure these rights, governments are instituted among men, deriving their just powers from the consent of the governed. We believe that whenever any form of government becomes destructive of these ends, it is the right of the people to alter or abolish it.

These words still resonate around the world today. People are sacrificing their lives just to have a chance to achieve this dream. They died at Tiananmen Square, they are dying in South Africa and Burma because they believe in government of the people, by the people, and for the people.

Yet in this country, where we receive that gift by birthright, we are in danger of letting the dream of self-government die through inattention, inanition, and the corruption of our political system by special-interest money. There has grown in our government a kind of carelessness about the requirements of the Constitution: Under the pressure of the cold war, our government has sometimes behaved as though the people had no business knowing what it was doing, as though the government were somehow separate from or above the people it was created to serve.

To run this government for the people of the United States is our goal. But self-government is a two-way street. Democracy requires that each citizen exercise his or her own civic responsibilities. Those responsibilities are many and varied; some we may choose among, and a few are forced upon us. We all have an obligation to obey the laws, but beyond that, we have obligations to one another. For democracy to work, the people must care about it and be involved in it. It is not enough to say "politics doesn't interest me" or "all politicians are crooks" and to dismiss it from your mind. We, the people, are all responsible for this country, and for the ideals of democracy for which it stands.

It is for us to be here rededicated to the unfinished task remaining before us: freedom and justice for all.

Fort Worth Star-Telegram, January 3, 1993

SLEAZY RIDERS

"Texas political ethics" is not an oxymoron. Our guys have 'em. They just tend to have an over-developed sense of the extenuating circumstance.

Remember when Bill Clements was asked why he'd lied about approving payments to Southern Methodist University football players and replied, "Well, there was never a Bible in the room . . ."? There was that to be considered, wasn't there?

Remember when a crusty state senator named Bill Moore was caught carrying a bill that would directly benefit his own company and said, "I'd just make a little bit of money, I wouldn't make a whole lot . . ."? You see? These things are complicated.

When you've got Louisiana on one side and Mexico on another, the sleaze standard is high, but we're holding our own. Look what became of the last six Speakers — three got indicted, two got defeated, one got shot. One of the indictees, Billy Clayton, got in trouble for taking five thousand dollars in cash from a lobbyist, which he said he meant to return, honest, but it just somehow slipped his mind. He got off. If there's one thing a Texas Speaker has got to know, it's how to explain himself.

The definitive statement on Texas political ethics — source unknown, but often quoted by Texas liberals — is: "If you can't take their money, drink their whiskey, screw their women, and vote against 'em anyway, you don't belong in the Legislature." But things are getting better. We seldom pay them off in cash anymore. They want their money the legal way, as campaign contributions.

In the not-so-distant past, they were more upfront about it. Two state senators were holed up in the Driskill Hotel, drinkin' whiskey and "interviewin' secretaries." Comes a *knock-knock-knock* on the door, and it's the lobbyist for the chiropractors. He offers both senators two hundred dollars to vote for the chiropractors' bill. One guy takes the money, the bill comes up, and lo and behold, he votes against it. This is bad Texas political ethics: You're supposed to stay bought. The chiropractor lobbyist is some pissed. He stalks up to the senator and demands to know what happened. "Doctors offered me four hundred to vote against you," said the senator. The lobbyist started to cuss that senator up one side and down the other. "Look," the senator argued, "you knew I was weak when I took the two hundred."

The late pol Woodrow Bean of El Paso, God rest him, used to tell the story of the time a court appointed him to defend a young robber who had made off with the loot with the cops right on his

284

heels. Woody interviews this kid in the hoosegow, gets the directions to where the loot is stashed, drives out there, and helps himself to a very generous fee. As he drives away, he says aloud, "Woodrow Wilson Bean, you are skatin' on the thin edge of ethics." Then he drives awhile further and says, "Woodrow Wilson Bean, ethics is for young lawyers."

Occasionally things get so bad that the press bestirs itself into a state of high dudgeon and the citizenry gets aroused. Then all the pols run for cover and talk about reform, only they pronounce it *"ree*-form," as in, "We're gonna have us some *ree*-form around here," just to let each other know they aren't really serious. Back in 1973, when they were supposed to be cleaning up the mess from the Sharpstown scandal, the House chamber was the scene of a performance by the Apache Belles from Tyler Junior College. The highlight came when six Belles turned their derrieres toward the lawmakers, revealing letters spelling out *R-E-F-O-R-M*. Texas voters, knowing better than to expect the Lege to put an end to sleaze, have resorted to their own ways of dealing with it, which sometimes take the form of voting half the Legislature out of office and more often result in electing folks who are god-awful rich in the hope that they or their ancestors have already stolen all they need.

But the scandals go on. Since Sharpstown we've had Brilab and Gibgate and a list of sleaze du jours too long to recount. Who can forget the time Bo Pilgrim, the East Texas chicken magnate, walked

285

onto the floor of the senate during a special session in 1989 and started handing out checks for ten thousand dollars — payee blank — to any senator who would take one? Seven took the money, but five gave it back when the story broke. Still, it was technically legit. That's Texas ethics for you. The real scandal isn't what's illegal — it's what's legal.

The Texas Observer, February 1993

LET GAYS SERVE THEIR COUNTRY AND GET ON TO REAL PROBLEMS

A letter writer points out something about the flap over homosexuals in the armed services that is so obvious everyone has overlooked it. It's the old saw about when you ask the wrong question, you get the wrong answer.

The question we've all been asking is: Should we allow gays in the military? But the real question is: Should we kick gays out of the military just for being gay?

The current policy is estimated to cost us $42 million a year ($28,000 to train a replacement for an enlisted man; $121,000 for an officer).

Why should we pay $42 million a year for an ineffective and unjust rule? Everyone agrees there are about the same percent of gays in the military as there are in life, largely because most eighteen-year-old gays who join the military hope it will "make a man" out of them. As a friend of mine observed sardonically, no one ever joined the Army to get a date.

So here they are, doing their jobs, we assume, at about the same rate of competence to incompetence as everyone else. As James T. Bush, a retired U.S. Navy captain, points out, the issue is not sexual orientation but sexual behavior; sexual harassment, inappropriate passes, attempted rape, are all offensive sexual behaviors whether one is gay or straight and should be punished. The ban on simply being gay is not part of some longstanding tradition. It was instituted by Ronald Reagan in 1982. We got along quite well without it until then. No one considered the Marine Corps a bunch of sissies in 1981. No one is proposing that gays in the military be cut any slack on their behavior. So, why should we waste all this money hunting down people who are doing a good job and offending no one?

I think it's a silly waste of money. And that little charmer is, of course, just one of the helpings on Mr. Clinton's plate these days. Taking a look at all the roundup of issues Clinton needs to address right off the bat would be enough to make me take to my bed with the vapors if I were Clinton. Bosnia, Somalia, Iraq, NAFTA, illegal Haitian immigrants, and the former Soviet Union are just for starters in foreign policy.

Then health care, welfare reform, balancing the budget with a middle-class tax break, Mrs. Baird's Peruvian housekeeper, several thousand people who think they deserve tickets to inaugural events and can't get them, staffing the White House, where to put Hillary's office, the flap about

Chelsea's school, low-cost housing, urban riots.

Sounds like an Excedrin headache to me. And that is not to mention the torrents of advice Clinton is getting about each and every one of these problems.

All things considered, I'm not sure the poor man is going to spend several days celebrating next week. He is said to be in mourning a bit for his simple life in Little Rock — being able to jog to the Y in the morning ("my blue-collar gym where there's nobody in bright spandex outfits") and the famous stop at McDonald's for coffee.

It does help one to understand why presidents retreat inside the infamous "bubble," the perennially guarded zone around a president no one can enter without screening. Clinton has been thinking about how to escape that bubble since at least last summer, plotting more bus trips and continuing to wade into crowds while the Secret Service guys get acid stomach. He may yet be grateful for the bubble.

George Bush got so notoriously out of touch with the common folks that he was amazed by a supermarket scanner. I doubt that having the president do his own laundry is a wise investment of presidential time. But I do hope he continues to patronize McDonald's. Jimmy Carter managed to take his daughter there occasionally, with no great harm done to the majesty of the office.

Perhaps I am placing too much importance on symbols, but I suspect there really is something insidious about limousines. The father of a friend of mine who is a country-western star (the son is, not the father) has observed the effects of being what he calls "part-time rich" on his son.

When the son is on tour, he has a limousine and hotel suites and people fawning on him. His father says the extent to which one comes to expect that, and to be put out having to shlump along in a Ford Escort, is amazing.

Even more insidious than the trappings of wealth and power is the sycophancy that surrounds powerful people. I suppose even close friends are hesitant to say to a president, "Boy, that sure was a lousy speech you just gave," but the multitudes of FOB's might consider rigorous honesty to be part of their service to the nation.

Of course, having a teenage child is quite useful for the purposes of keeping down the inflation of self-esteem. So are newspaper columnists.

Fort Worth Star-Telegram, January 17, 1993

PURE DELIGHT 101

One way we know this is a great nation is because, now that the Elvis stamp is finally out, thousands of our fellow citizens are sticking it on letters and deliberately misaddressing them so they will come back stamped RETURN TO SENDER.

Another reason we know we're a great nation is because the Lawn Chair Precision Drill Team was the biggest hit of the inaugural parade of our forty-second president. Two items roughly the equivalent of "From the halls of Montezuma to the shores of Tripoli," no?

Personally, I had a swell time at Bill Clinton's inaugural shindig and am a bit puzzled as to why so many of my journalistic brethren appeared to be attending a different event. The political press corps seems to be having a bumpy transition. I would be consoled if I thought their grumpiness, pettiness, and general mumpishness about this new administration were only a commendable counterreaction to the excessive bum-kissing displayed by a few of the brethren; better grump than suck up, I always say. But I am afraid many of my colleagues are motivated by something other than a desire to avoid sycophancy.

Maureen Dowd of *The New York Times*, whose style I have always liked, opined on a radio talk show, "Well. If the Clinton administration can re-create itself, then perhaps we'll remember this period as just a bad dream." Personally, I think calling on an administration to re-create itself before it has even been sworn in is a trifle premature.

Having called for Zoë Baird's head, or at least her withdrawal, several days before anyone else in the press seemed to notice there was a problem with her, I was surprised — you can imagine how surprised — when the rest of the gang joined me, milling about in an inchoate rage about yuppie crimes, class distinctions, offensive pretense to moral purity, and a bunch of other stuff that didn't have dog to do with exploiting illegal workers. "Gee," said I, "??????!"

Beyond that, any group of ink-stained wretches who could fail to appreciate the beauty of Arkansans in D.C. needs to be sent back for remedial work in Pure Delight 101. The Arkies swarmed all over the capital, wearing they razorback-hog helmets on they un-pointy heads and bellowing, "Soooooooie-pig!" every two minutes. In the first place, any group of folks willing to make asses of themselves in pursuit of a good time should be commended and encouraged: The spirit of human frolic needs all the help it can get. Numero two-o, for once those making too much noise and having too much fun were not Texans, a source of solace for those of us who have single-handedly represented National Vulgarity all these years.

I was a little startled when the moment came for the swearing in and I learned we were getting William Jefferson Clinton as president: We're so accustomed to his "Bill," who knew he was WJC? But as a *New Yorker* cartoon suggested, had we stuck with the informal all along, history would have given us Bill Henry Harrison, Bill McKinley, and Bill Howard Taft.

In principle, I disapprove of the entire inaugural do — if you are going to raise $30 million from assorted corporate sources, there are better things to do with it than hold a three-day party. On the other hand, if you're going to hold a three-day party that costs 30 million bucks, you ought, by God, to enjoy it.

The Progressive, March 1991

BEWARE THOSE WHO PROFIT FROM FEAR

On what we trust will be a sunny Sunday, religion is on my mind. In particular, what appears to be an increasingly respectable form of bigotry these days: antifundamentalism.

William Martin of Rice University, sociologist of religion and biographer of Billy Graham, points out that what happens as a society becomes more modern and more secular is that those who hew to conservative, traditional values start clinging to them more tenaciously and vociferously. Because they feel more and more threatened by the pace of change in society, their conservatism and traditionalism becomes more extreme.

What begins as a gap between the two groups grows into a chasm.

I am no doubt doing damage to Martin's thesis by oversimplifying it, but I believe this is what is happening in our society.

The aggravation of the distance between modernists and traditionalists is worsened by that usual suspect — the media.

In trying to think of a recent movie, television show, or book in which the protagonist is a sympathetically portrayed fundamentalist, I have come up with one: a love of a little novel called *Raney* by Clyde Edgerton. (Of course, Edgerton was fired from his teaching job at a fundamentalist school after the book came out because there's some mild sex in it, but these things do happen.)

Intellectuals in America have traditionally despised fundamentalists; H. L. Mencken on the subject of "wowsers" is still corrosively funny. As it happens, I was born and raised amongst footwashin' Baptists myself, so I have never regarded them as peculiar. I got saved three times before I was twelve. It didn't take in the long run, but I hold that it did me no harm.

My ambivalence about fundamentalist Christians stems from their role in politics. I have always subscribed to the philosophy of Mr. Dooley, the great sage of Chicago, who once inquired, "Is there, in all the history of human folly, a greater fool than a clergyman in politics?"

The politicization of fundamentalists, first seen in the mid-1970s in the form of the Moral Majority, has proceeded until now these Shiite Baptists are simply running amok in politics.

Given the state of politics in this country, any reasonable person is entitled to conclude that politics could use an injection of the Good Book. But we are witnessing instead the very sort of divisive, doctrinal disputation — the insistence that all citizens behave according to the beliefs of some —

that led our Founding Fathers to the doctrine of separation of church and state at the beginning of this nation.

I have recently noticed a number of misexplanations of separation of church and state being spread by fundamentalists. "It's not in the Constitution," they cry. Actually, it is, even though the words "separation of church and state" do not appear therein.

The Establishment Clause of the First Amendment is what separates church and state. The Founders were perfectly clear about what they were doing. It was put best by James Madison, in that magnificent eighteenth-century prose of which we are no longer capable: The purpose of the separation of church and state "is to keep forever from these shores the ceaseless strife that has soaked the soil of Europe in blood for centuries."

And still does. In Bosnia, a considerable amount of that blood reportedly comes from Moslem virgins who are raped as a matter of policy by their Serbian Christian neighbors.

To understand the fears of fundamentalists is to understand their foolishness. But they get precious little understanding, not to mention empathy or sympathy, from those who pride themselves on their compassion.

Fear is the most dangerous emotion in politics. People do terrible things to one another out of fear. In my opinion, anyone who can look at the raunchier frontiers of American culture without at least some trepidation hasn't got a lick of sense.

But we are now looking at a form of fundamentalism in which fear is being deliberately fanned for political purposes.

The boogeymen are everywhere: Sex education will lead to promiscuity, AIDS, and Chinese communism. Failure to discriminate against gay people will lead to Sodom and Gomorrah. Failure to have official prayers in school means the End Is Nigh.

I have no claim to expertise on eternal rewards and punishments. But personally, I suspect there is a special place in hell for the fear-mongers.

Fort Worth Star-Telegram, February 28, 1993

GATHER A FEW TEXANS TOGETHER, AND THERE HIS GREAT SPIRIT WILL BE ALSO

Sam Houston's birthplace near Lexington, Va. — A hardy crew of Houston-lovers gathered here on the two hundredth birthday of the Greatest Texan to pay their respects and keep vigil on the rocky ridge in the Shenandoah Valley where Sam was born on the date he later ensured would become Texas Independence Day.

Actually, we hoped that Sam's ghost might appear.

We commenced our vigil just before midnight, standing in the snow around a hardwood fire (enough to make one yearn for the burning properties of Texas cedar), and told tales of Houston until four A.M. The hard core stayed up till five-thirty. No ghost was sighted, but I rather think the spirit of Houston joined us that night as, medicinally ingesting cognac to keep our feet warm, we were inspired to top one another with story after story of Sam's freedom-fighting and fun-making.

Texans revere Sam Houston because he was, quite simply, a great man. His courage, his integrity and his sense of honor were as outsize as Houston himself. And physically, he was a giant of a man.

But Texans relish and cherish Houston for his foibles, not his virtues. He has always seemed to me to be the most human of our great men — the kind of man any one of us would adore to have over for dinner or to spend an evening with. The Raven. Big Drunk. General.

As a young man in Tennessee, Houston, a lawyer at the time, was part of a short-lived theatrical company, playing villains, heroes, and — an especially memorable performance — a drunken porter. The director of the company said, "I never met a man who had a keener sense of the ridiculous."

What a lovely quality. And look how well it served him in the course of a life more melodramatic than any of the lurid dramas so beloved in nineteenth-century America. Houston once passed one of his pompous political enemies on the street. The fellow said, "I, sir, do not speak to scoundrels!"

Sam replied, "Ah, well, you see that I do."

Our crew of Houston-lovers, convened by former state senator Don Kennard of Fort Worth, included former representative Bob Eckhardt of Houston, a true Houston scholar, and representatives John Bryant of Dallas and Bill Sarpalius of Amarillo, both aficionados of the great man, plus a scattering of all-purpose Texas miscreants.

Kennard, who has spent a lifetime in and around politics, observed at one point that perhaps the most unusual thing about Houston was that although he frankly burned with ambition — oh, he yearned to make his mark — he never behaved selfishly to do so.

"Many men with ambition are willing to step on and even trample over others in their climb," said Kennard, "but Houston never did that. He had great ambition, but he never did in anyone else in order to get ahead."

I suppose we all see in Houston what we would most like to see in ourselves. For myself, I love him most for what he hated: injustice, bigotry, pomposity, snobbery, and hypocrisy.

I think of Sam Houston as the first professional Texan, always prepared to gross out stuffy Easterners obsessed with petty proprieties.

Houston was once seated next to a starchy dame at a state banquet. They were served burning-hot soup. After taking a spoonful, Houston promptly spat it out all over the tablecloth and then said to his horrified dining companion, "You know, if I were a damn fool, I would have swallowed that."

One reason we all admire Sam is because he waited until quite late in his life to reform, and even then, you could never be sure it had taken all the way. His wife, Margaret, got him started on the Baptist road to virtue, and when at last he lay dying, she suggested he call in all his old enemies one by one for forgiveness and Christian fellowship. This program went along swimmingly until Margaret said, "Don't you think it's time to call in Lamar?" Houston hated Mirabeau B. Lamar, whom he persisted in calling "Miraboo," because when Lamar was an Indian agent, he acted treacherously to take advantage of the Indians, something Houston could never forgive. Houston told his wife, "When I am dead, you can call in Lamar, turn me over, and tell him to kiss my cold ass."

In all that extraordinary life of triumph and tragedy, it seems to me the greatest, the most heroic moment was the one many still think of as the lowest point: the long night before they would have forced him to take the oath of secession and join the Confederacy when Houston knew he would be driven from office. How magnificently the words he wrote that night in his "Letter to the People of Texas" still ring:

Fellow-Citizens, in the name of your rights and liberties, which I believe have been trampled upon, I refuse to take this oath. In the name of the nationality of Texas, which has been betrayed by the Convention, I refuse to take this oath. In the name of the Constitution of Texas, which has been trampled upon, I refuse to take this oath. In the name of my own conscience and manhood, which this Convention would degrade by dragging me before it, to pander to the malice

301

of my enemies, I refuse to take this oath.

I am ready to be ostracized sooner than submit to usurpation. Office has no charm for me, that it must be purchased at the sacrifice of my conscience, and the loss of my self-respect.

I love Texas too well to bring civil strife and bloodshed upon her. To avert this calamity, I shall make no endeavor to maintain my authority as Chief Executive of this State.

It is perhaps but meet that my career should close thus. I have seen the patriots and statesmen of my youth, one by one, gathered to their fathers, and the Government which they created, rent in twain; and none like them are left to unite it once again. I am the last almost of a race, who learned from their lips the lessons of human freedom. I am stricken down now, because I will not yield those principles, which I have fought for and struggled to maintain. The severest pang is that the blow comes in the name of Texas.

His motto was: Do right, and risk consequences.

Fort Worth Star-Telegram, March 4, 1993

PRESS PACK'S YAMMERING GROWS OLD

I believe one should never pass up an opportunity to berate the Washington press corps, and so I did the other night.

Now that I've gotten all that spleen out of my system, it occurs to me I was a little unfair — just a trifle, you understand. I probably shouldn't have referred to the White House press corps as "a bunch of trained seals sitting around waiting for their four o'clock feeding."

Just because we read more about Hillary's hat than about homelessness was no reason for me to take the press corps on in that tacky fashion, was it?

In the calmer light of day, it occurs to me that my brethren and sistren in this trade are just trying to make up for lost time. Having blown every big story of the eighties — including Iran-*contra*, Iraqgate, S&Ls, Reaganomics, and the HUD scandal, just to mention a few — my colleagues are now determined to play "gotcha" journalism with the Clinton administration. Who am I to plead with the brethren, "Jeez, give the guy a break."

I don't believe in breaks for the powerful, never have. And by George, that inaugural hat of Hillary's was silly looking.

The reason I avoid Washington as much as possible is not because this is a city where everybody says what everybody else says. It's because whenever I'm here for ten minutes, I find myself saying exactly what everybody else says. Which is why I'm writing about Hillary Rodham Clinton and her hat.

The latest flap about Clinton is that she won't open the policy-making process on health care to the press. Now, I'm confused about this. I thought I knew what secret government was. Ten years of covering Gib Lewis, and I know a done deal when I see one. I just finished lambasting Bob Bullock for calling in the special interests to cut a deal on products liability. And now here's the Washington press corps agog because Clinton isn't calling in lobbyists for the American Medical Association to get their input on the health-care plan. Uh. Excuse me. But, why should she?

Doesn't she get to work on her proposal without the press and the lobsters at the table? Isn't the usual deal that after she finishes this proposal and releases it, then the press and the lobsters pick it apart?

I've no objection to the press picking on the Clinton administration — have at 'em — but I think the press has come down with a bad case of premature picking.

I recall Abe Rosenthal, then managing editor of *The New York Times* and, Lord knows, not a man I often agreed with, once mildly suggesting that the new mayor of New York should be given a chance to mess up before we attacked him. In that particular case (Ed Koch), I thought we held off far too long, but I agreed with Abe's premise.

Quite a disconcerting number of the brethren here were claiming that the Clinton administration was a disaster before the man had even been sworn in.

I am puzzled by the Washington press corps's reaction to affirmative action by the Clinton administration — not reverse discrimination, but affirmative action.

I thought it was a good idea to have an administration that "looks like America" instead of the usual suits. Look what's already happening on the Hill now that it looks a little more like the rest of America. When the family leave bill was being debated, Senator Patty Murray of Washington, the "mom in tennis shoes," put in her oar by recalling when she had to quit her secretarial job because she got pregnant.

When they were discussing the Zoë Baird problem of people not paying Social Security taxes on their domestic workers, Representative Carrie Meek of Florida allowed as how she had been a domestic worker at one point in her life, and her mom was a domestic worker and so were all her sisters. Not a point of view normally heard in the corridors of power from the suits.

I am uneasily reminded of the last time this press corps failed to understand a president (for kindness' sake, we will draw a veil over the performance of this press corps during the Reagan years). Jimmy Carter was a president the press just never cottoned to. Like the senators during the Anita Hill–Clarence Thomas hearings, they just didn't get it.

Actually, it was pretty simple. Jimmy Carter has been out of office for thirteen years now. And every day for thirteen years, that man has gone out and behaved like a good Christian — for no money. Because that's who he is, and that's who he always was. But that was too simple for Power Town.

Fort Worth Star-Telegram, March 7, 1993

GET A KNIFE, GET A DOG,
BUT GET RID OF GUNS

Guns. Everywhere guns.

Let me start this discussion by pointing out that I am not antigun. I'm pro-knife. Consider the merits of the knife.

In the first place, you have to catch up with someone in order to stab him. A general substitution of knives for guns would promote physical fitness. We'd turn into a whole nation of great runners. Plus, knives don't ricochet. And people are seldom killed while cleaning their knives.

As a civil libertarian, I, of course, support the Second Amendment. And I believe it means exactly what it says:

A well-regulated militia being necessary to the security of a free state, the right of the people to keep and bear arms shall not be infringed. Fourteen-year-old boys are not part of a well-regulated militia. Members of wacky religious cults are not part of a well-regulated militia. Permitting unregulated citizens to have guns is destroying the security of this free state.

I am intrigued by the arguments of those who claim to follow the judicial doctrine of original intent. How do they know it was the dearest wish of Thomas Jefferson's heart that teenage drug dealers should cruise the cities of this nation perforating their fellow citizens with assault rifles? Channeling?

There is more hooey spread about the Second Amendment. It says quite clearly that guns are for those who form part of a well-regulated militia, that is, the armed forces, including the National Guard. The reasons for keeping them away from everyone else get clearer by the day.

The comparison most often used is that of the automobile, another lethal object that is regularly used to wreak great carnage. Obviously, this society is full of people who haven't enough common sense to use an automobile properly. But we haven't outlawed cars yet.

We do, however, license them and their owners, restrict their use to presumably sane and sober adults, and keep track of who sells them to whom. At a minimum, we should do the same with guns.

In truth, there is no rational argument for guns in this society. This is no longer a frontier nation in which people hunt their own food. It is a crowded, overwhelmingly urban country in which letting people have access to guns is a continuing disaster. Those who want guns — whether for target shooting, hunting, or potting rattlesnakes (get a hoe) — should be subject to the same restrictions placed on gun owners in England, a nation in which liberty has survived nicely without an armed populace.

The argument that "guns don't kill people" is patent nonsense. Anyone who has ever worked in a cop shop knows how many family arguments end in murder because there was a gun in the house. Did the gun kill someone? No. But if there had been no gun, no one would have died. At least not without a good foot race first. Guns do kill. Unlike cars, that is all they do.

Michael Crichton makes an interesting argument about technology in his thriller *Jurassic Park*. He points out that power without discipline is making this society into a wreckage. By the time someone who studies the martial arts becomes a master — literally able to kill with bare hands — that person has also undergone years of training and discipline. But any fool can pick up a gun and kill with it.

"A well-regulated militia" surely implies both long training and long discipline. That is the least, the very least, that should be required of those who are permitted to have guns, because a gun is literally the power to kill. For years I used to enjoy taunting my gun-nut friends about their psychosexual hang-ups — always in a spirit of good cheer, you understand. But letting the noisy minority in the NRA force us to allow this carnage to continue is just plain insane.

I do think gun nuts have a power hang-up. I don't know what is missing in their psyches that they need to feel they have the power to kill. But

no sane society would allow this to continue.
Ban the damn things. Ban them all.
You want protection? Get a dog.

Fort Worth Star-Telegram, March 9, 1993

CISNEROS'S CROSS

Billie Carr, the mother of Texas liberal politics, often says, "All politicians are alligators; they are *all* alligators." But I'm putting on the line twenty-five years' worth of membership in good standing as a skeptic, if not a cynic, to warn you to expect more from Henry Cisneros, now secretary of Housing and Urban Development in Clinton's cabinet. This one is a human being.

He's a tall, handsome Mexican-American with, at this point, a fairly tortured soul. Charisma, class, stage presence — whatever you call it, Cisneros has it. On his bad days, he's an excellent public speaker; on his good days, he's electrifying. He is remarkably bright, but unlike many very bright people, he is patient with those who are not. He is an idealist tempered by fifteen years in the maw of big-city politics, an academic tempered by real-world experience.

For all that, Cisneros has just made what I think is a major mistake by taking the cabinet job. It's not that he'll disappear into the fog of the D.C. alphabet. No, you'll see Cisneros in every ghetto and barrio in the country and on MTV as well.

But he could have set his own agenda as the first Chicano U.S. senator from Texas, and who knows what after that?

The choice Cisneros made tells a lot about what it means to be both a human being and a politician in our time.

Cisneros, forty-five, comes from the West Side of San Antonio, the nation's tenth-largest city. His family is middle-class Mexican, people with great faith in education and hard work. Cisneros went to Central High with, among others, Ernesto Cortes, who later created a powerful Chicano organization in San Antonio.

Cisneros went on to Texas A&M, which makes him a Texas oddity: Chicano Aggies are fairly rare — though we expect to see more of them as a result of Cisneros's term as regent, when he instituted an effective affirmative action program. On scholarship, he attended graduate school at A&M, where he got a master's degree in urban and regional planning, then received another master's from Harvard and a doctorate from George Washington University, both in public administration. He worked in the San Antonio city manager's office for a few years, got elected to the city council in 1975, and became mayor in 1981.

HUD watchers should note that while Cisneros was mayor, $200 million was spent on the West Side for streets, gutters, libraries, and parks. The West Side used to be a sewer, literally: Its dirt streets flooded every time there was a heavy rain.

Ernie Cortes's group held Cisneros to his promises. It is sometimes said that Cortes is Cisneros's "good angel," perched on his shoulder, urging him to do what's right. His "bad angel" is an improbably cherubic political consultant named George Shipley, known as Doctor Dirt, who keeps urging Cisneros to run for whatever higher office opens up.

Cisneros was good, very good indeed, at getting disparate groups in the city to work together on economic development projects, such as Sea World, though he may have overreached himself on his last venture, the state-of-the-art Alamodome.

The mayor of San Antonio is paid $50 plus expenses per council meeting, period. Cisneros made a living during those years by teaching and speaking at college campuses. He and his wife, Mary Alice (a smart political campaigner in her own right), and children lived in a small house on the West Side. After fifteen years of public service Cisneros needed to make money: He had one daughter preparing to go to college, with another not far behind, and a one-year-old son, John Paul (named after the pope), with a serious congenital heart defect.

When John Paul had been born, it was understood that he would have to undergo several major surgeries, and even so was likely to die at age five or six. Henry and Mary Alice were devastated. John Paul's only hope was for medical advances. (It's still a hope — John Paul is to undergo surgery

313

again in May.) Henry C. (called so in San Antonio to distinguish him from the fighting congressman, Henry B. Gonzales) quit politics to make money. He'd also fallen in love.

The lady in question was Linda Medlar, a blond, Anglo fundraiser, beautiful and smart. Cisneros admitted the affair, which was common gossip in San Antonio. He might have used the "none of your business" answer, which advisers urged on him, had the affair been only a fling with some bimbette. But here were two adults with a genuine attraction for one another. The affair reinforced all the sorry old stereotypes about macho Latinos, and caused real grief and pain to thousands of Chicanas who had hero-worshipped Henry C.

Meanwhile, Mary Alice, under the stress of John Paul's illness, had taken up with a fundamentalist faith healer, believed by many to be a Rasputin-like figure. Mary Alice would take the baby to the faith healer's church, and he would put hands on the child before the congregation while everyone prayed.

Even in the midst of all the uproar, Cisneros remained popular, and many wanted him to run for governor in 1990. He decided not to, and his mentor Ann Richards ran instead. When she won, using the slogan the "New Texas," Cisneros was as excited as if he had won himself, envisioning an end to the corrupt, racist politics that had marred the state for so long. When Richards promised in her inaugural address that no Texas baby born with health problems would die for lack of medical care, tears poured down Cisneros's face.

While Cisneros was salting away money running an asset management company, he continued to be a major political player. He and Medlar parted after the publicity about their affair, and she moved to Lubbock. But the Cisneros marriage was still rocky. In 1992, Cisneros campaigned for Clinton, wowing the press as usual. After the election, Clinton wanted Cisneros for the cabinet and Richards wanted him for the Senate seat left vacant by Lloyd Bentsen's appointment to Treasury. The two of them played tug-of-war across Cisneros's tortured conscience.

He was a natural for the Senate — a Chicano Aggie who works well with business interests. But the special election is to be held in May, just when John Paul has to undergo surgery again. If the boy were to die, Cisneros wasn't sure he could handle it while in the public eye — wasn't sure he could handle it, period. Richards played hardball, telling him he'd have to want it more than anything in the world.

Cisneros kept saying that the HUD job was the one he is trained for and knows how to do. But won't the credit ultimately go to Bill Clinton? And didn't his hero Ann Richards need him?

It seesawed crazily back and forth. At one point, a Democratic political operative was told that the Republicans had film footage of Mary Alice and the baby with the faith healer and would use it against Cisneros if he ran for Senate. "Great!" crowed the op. "I'll have the first philandering

315

mackerel-snapper in history to get the fundamentalist vote!"

All the crushing considerations of running for office finally tipped the scales — seeing the affair dredged up again in the face of his still-fragile marriage; needing to raise $5 million for the race and having to run again in two years; and most of all, John Paul. Against that was the chance to do a job he's been training for all his life, a chance to help the poor and oppressed of the great cities, a chance to make reparation for the harm he felt he had done to his name, to his family, and to his race by falling in love. Like a regular person.

No wonder so many politicians seem like alligators.

Mother Jones, March/April 1993

'TWAS A FINE SPRING DAY TO AIR OUT ATTITUDES

Well, the gay folks had a fine march in Washington, D.C., but I think they missed a couple of bets. State senator Jack Gordon of Florida suggests that they should have stopped en route and had a ceremony thanking the feds for naming that fine new building right there on Pennsylvania Avenue after one of their own. That's the J. Edgar Hoover Building.

Speaking of whom, there was a great example of why we don't want to force gays to stay in the closet.

And I would have liked to have seen a banner reading, BAN HETEROSEXUALS FROM THE MILITARY — REMEMBER TAILHOOK. I trust you all took a look at the charming little report on that incident.

I suspect that finally ventilating all the myths and misconceptions about gays is a useful exercise, even for those who would prefer not to think about them. "I have nothing against gays," my mother is fond of saying. "I just wish they'd stay in the closet." But we all know by now — or should

— that that state of affairs was cruel and unjust and led to terrible abuses.

Of all the odd misperceptions current about homosexuality, perhaps the oddest is that it is a choice, that people choose to be homosexual. That strikes me as so patently silly. Did any of us who are straight choose to be heterosexual? When? Did we wake up one morning when we were fifteen and say, "Gosh, I think I'll be a heterosexual"? For heaven's sakes, how can anyone believe that people choose to be homosexual? "I think it would be a lot of fun to be called *queer* and *sissy* for the rest of my life, so I think I'll be gay."

Last time I checked, the experts were still leaning toward the view that homosexuality is multi-causational (isn't that a dandy word?). Most gay people I know believe they were literally born that way, that it's like being left-handed or brown-eyed. But in at least some cases, there is apparently some developmental influence as well.

The best description I ever heard of sexual orientation came from Dr. John Money of The Johns Hopkins University, who used to draw it on a horizontal scale going from one to ten, with one being completely homosexual and ten being completely heterosexual. Money says that very few people are either one or ten and about as few are at five (totally bisexual). Most of us fall into a clump ranging from about six to eight, while there's a smaller clump of homosexuals ranging from about four to two.

Because homosexuality occurs in many species of animals (stickleback fish always struck me as the strangest case) and because it has appeared in all human cultures throughout history, we must conclude that it is what statisticians call a "normal aberrant" (and isn't that a dandy phrase?).

I actually saw a letter to the editor last week declaring that homosexuality is a symptom of the decadence and decline of civilization and that it didn't exist among primitive people such as American Indians. *Au contraire,* as we say in Lubbock. Aside from the insult to Indians, there were indeed gay Indians before the white man came, and at least in the Plains tribes, they were regarded as sort of endearingly special.

Among the less charming counterdemonstrators at the Washington march was the group from Kansas carrying signs saying, GOD HATES FAGS and DEATH TO FAGS. It is true that the Old Testament contains an injunction against homosexuality; it's in the same list of laws given when the Hebrews were a wandering desert people and were forbidden to eat shellfish. I always thought Christians were supposed to be followers of Jesus Christ, and Jesus' injunctions to love one another — to love even the despised and the outcast — could scarcely be clearer. Hate is not a Christian value.

And, of course, there are the gay fundamentalists. We all know of scandals involving gay preachers, and if you wonder what it's like to

319

grow up gay in a religious environment that stigmatizes gays, I commend to you a truly funny book called *Strange Angel — The Gospel According to Benny Joe* by Ben Davis, who grew up near Dallas and would have become a fundamentalist preacher had it not been for his sexual orientation. The book's affectionate look at fundamentalist religion is worth the price for that alone (it is published by Corona Publishing, San Antonio).

As a matter of law, I do not see that we have any choice but to seek to ensure that gays have full civil rights. They are citizens; they pay taxes; as Jesse Jackson said the day of the march, no one gives them a break on April 15. They serve honorably in the military, ban or no ban; the Sixth Army's soldier of the year marched Sunday in Washington.

It has been my observation that some gay people are absolutely wonderful human beings, and some are complete you-know-whats, and most are somewhere in between. Depressingly like heterosexuals. So I suggest we all grow up and get over our small-town prejudices. (I can never remember whether it was "Queers wear red on Friday" or "green on Thursday." Lord, didn't we grow up with some silly ideas?) In our fair land, no one can force us to be tolerant. But neither can prejudice be allowed to keep people out of jobs for which they are qualified.

I suppose some people will continue to feel entitled to hate gays. As the psychiatrists have been telling us for a long time, hating them seems to be a function of being afraid that you might be one yourself.

Fort Worth Star-Telegram, April 27, 1993

DEBATERS OF SEX-ED BILL, TAKE A BOW

If you take the cheerful view, as I do, that anything that gets people involved in the political system — gets 'em out there exercising their rights, giving their elected representatives what-for, generally putting their oar in, no matter how misguided they may be — then Thursday's Senate hearing on sex education was a Good Thing.

Unfortunately, the good guys lost: The sex-ed bill has been referred to subcommittee, never to see the light of day, and the epidemic of teenage pregnancy in Texas will continue.

Apart from the unfortunate outcome, it was a dandy show. We had people lambasting sin, people supporting secondary virginity, people declaring that the trouble with Senate Bill 20 is that God is not in control, and people who lumped self-esteem with out-of-body experiences. We heard from people who blame the liberal media, people who blame the 1960s, people who blame Satanists, and people who blame sex education for sex. We got prescriptions for abstinence, more Jesus, and just telling minors that sex is illegal.

All in all, it was the damnedest mishmash you ever heard. The total effect was not unlike reading several issues of the *National Enquirer* back-to-back: By the time you got through, you had no idea what to believe, a general sense that the world is going to hell on a sled, and absolutely nothing could surprise you.

My favorite bone of contention du jour was the matter of misinformation. "We have heard several references to 'misinformation' being spread by opponents of Senate Bill 20," some opponent would begin, and then go on to assure us that he or she had nothing but the straight-straight. And then follow that with still more stunning untruths. One woman declared that there had been two court decisions prompted by the American Civil Liberties Union holding that teaching abstinence is a violation of the separation of church and state (I checked with both reputed locales of such decisions — no such thing.)

So many untruths were told about the Sex Information and Education Council of the U.S., or SIECUS, that the outfit is now threatening to file a libel suit against the Texas Council on Family Values.

I was struck by the level of paranoia of the opponents — their fear not of what was in the bill, not of what they could see in writing, but their fear of what might be. SB 20 clearly says that local school boards may develop their own sex-ed curriculums and that parents may opt their kids out of sex-ed classes. For some reason, neither provision made any impression on the opponents, who kept insisting that local school boards and parents would be powerless to prevent their kids from being taught any number of things the parents hold repugnant. "Must we talk to them about masturbation?" plaintively inquired one witness.

"I have no objection to the central elements of the bill," said a minister from the Big Sandy Church of Christ, "but look down the road to what might be taught."

Lest all this sound like a long, depressing parade of unclear thinking, the beauty of the hearing — and of the involvement of real people as opposed to the crowds of $400 suits and tassel loafers that show up for most hearings — was that by the end of the long, long day, I really think most of those who attended, both for and against teaching sex education, had gained some respect for the integrity of the concern that motivated their opponents. No one is happy about the rising tide of teen pregnancy. The utter divergence of opinion on what to do about it should not be allowed to obscure the development of that basic democratic prerequisite for any solution: recognition that your opponents are not evil, even if they are misguided.

A big hand to all who turned out to show their concern, and to the senators who listened to it all.

My own favorite testimony came from Dr. Edward Tyson of Austin, who specializes in adolescent medicine and spoke for the Texas Medical

Association. Opponents of the bill constantly reiterated that condoms sometimes fail and that only abstinence is infallible for preventing both pregnancy and sexually transmitted diseases.

In response, Tyson said: "In the literature, there is a paucity of evidence that advocating abstinence prevents pregnancy. Ask anyone how many people they know who didn't intend to have sex but wound up having it anyway. Vows of abstinence fail far more often than condoms. And 'Just say no' has done as much for drugs and sex as 'Have a nice day' has for depression."

Fort Worth Star-Telegram, April 4, 1993

STOP AND SMELL THE ROSES

State representative Sergio Muñoz of Mission, Texas, got arrested the other day for possession of 626 pounds of marijuana. Well, nobody's perfect.

The seventy-third session of the Texas Legislature is in full roar and no one's life, liberty, or property is safe. Senator Bill Sims of San Angelo has introduced a bill that would create a cause of legal action against anyone who says disparaging things about Texas fruits or vegetables. I don't know. Maybe he just wants to get back at George Bush for trashing broccoli.

More comprehensible is Representative Todd Hunter's bill that would make the planned, organized release of balloons a Class C misdemeanor. (Exceptions for meteorological or scientific balloons but not for trial balloons.) Turns out there's a vogue for releasing balloons at memorial services, and the deflated balloons have been found gagging sea turtles. "Better to bust a funeral than choke a Kemp's Ridley," one environmentalist told *The Texas Observer*. And you thought our solons faced no tough choices.

We have the usual number of bills that would impose the death penalty for this, that, and the other. We've got one to castrate repeat sex offenders and another that would permit Texans to carry concealed handguns. All in all, we're chugging along with our normal *je ne sais quoi*. Except for poor ol' Mike Moncrief, a senator from Fort Worth, who has introduced a sex-education bill.

Moncrief, one of the world's squarest people, now finds himself denounced as a tool of Satan and even as the Arch-Fiend himself. Actually, he does have a mustache. The "People Against Smiling," as they are known around the Capitol — Shiite Baptists stirred up by their fundamentalist mullahs — have been descending upon us in droves, with Bibles in hand and abstinence as their cry. Representative Leticia Van De Putte is voting with Moncrief. She decided teenage pregnancy was a real problem when she found a twenty-four-year-old grandfather in her district.

I know. You're all dying to hear about the Texas Stand-Off, a story so big it now has its own television logo. One of my colleagues who is gay was dispatched to the front in Waco, the Vatican City of the Baptists, and reports that he located a gay sub-sect of the Koresh cult. He claims they call themselves the Brunch Davidians, believe that Jesus died on a croissant, and are inclined to carry on about it. I doubt this, myself.

What can I tell you? The Koreshies had broken

no laws before the BATF came bursting in with guns blazing. The petty, parochial, jurisdictional disputes among the lawmen in Waco are enough to choke a roach. The Texas Rangers were finally called in after the FBI. Which reminds me of the Ranger who once opined, "Son, the three most overrated things on earth are young pussy, Mack trucks, and the FBI."

At $2 million a day, we think it would be cheaper just to build a big fence around the Koresh complex, declare it a prison, and have all the cops leave. All around the complex, agents are cutting book deals and movie deals. I say, can the FBI's hostage negotiating team and call in the real pros from Hollywood. Bring in Michael Ovitz: "Davey, baby, I can get you five percent of the gross and a million up front." Around Waco these days, "the gross" is king.

Aside from that, we're all fine. It's springtime in Texas. The bluebonnets and the Indian paintbrush are out in South Texas, the occatillo is unfurling its red flags in the Big Bend, and the whoopers are back on the Gulf Coast. The cattle have calved, the redbud's blooming in Austin, and the little-yellows — we have more than six hundred varieties of small yellow wildflowers here so no one ever bothers to learn their names — are showing up in the Panhandle. While the East Coast went through the Great Blizzard of '93, the zone-tail hawks soared in our clear blue skies, still and steady on the updrafts and playing tag on the downs. The horses are frisky, it's up to eighty in the afternoons, and the lush green that follows a rainy winter here carpets the Great State.

May spring be upon you, too.

The Progressive, May 1993

THE KORESH TRAGEDY

If anyone can think of anything good to say about law enforcement's handling of the Branch Davidians from beginning to end, please call. I'm stumped.

We're looking at eighty-seven people dead, seventeen of them children, and for what? What did those kids ever do to anybody?

The fact that David Koresh sexually abused young girls is now being used to justify the cremation of eighty-seven people. But you will recall that all this started as an operation by the Bureau of Alcohol, Tobacco, and Firearms, which does not handle child abuse cases, and now we know why. Nor is the BATF assigned to monitor poor nutrition or lack of sanitation, which Attorney General Janet Reno cited as reasons for the final disastrous raid on the Koresh compound. Child abuse is supposed to be handled by social workers, not gun-toters.

The rationale for the original assault on Koresh was that a religious nut had assembled a large arsenal of dangerous weapons. Fine. Just one problem. It was all *legal*. Let me run that by you again:

Every weapon Koresh bought, he bought legally from a licensed firearms dealer. No, I don't think it is a good idea for a lunatic to have a huge weapons cache. But if we wanted to do something about it, we should have changed the law, right?

And if the Bureau of ATF wanted to chat with Koresh about his plans for that arsenal, there was an easy solution. Koresh was taped talking to a government negotiator after the initial raid. "Like I say, it would've been better if you just called me up or talked to me. Then you all could have come in and done your work." Both the McLennan County sheriff and the former district attorney say that whenever they wanted to talk to Koresh, they just called him up and asked him to come down to their offices. He was around town regularly. He went out for hamburgers, he went out to buy the kids Ski-Do's and go-carts. It wasn't impossible or even difficult to find him. The classic method of catching a nut, if you think you have to catch him, is to drop a net over him. What you don't do is mount an enormous armed assault on the place where you know the nut has his weapons stored. Unless, of course, you're the Bureau of Alcohol, Tobacco, and Firearms and you're worried that your budget is going to be slashed under a new administration and you want to make a big splash.

Enthusiasts of law and order now say Koresh should have accepted the warrant ATF came to serve on him. The same enthusiasts of law and order believe the man in Louisiana who shot an unarmed Japanese exchange student just for approaching his home was justified. ATF agents approached the Koresh compound with guns blazing: Under Texas law, you're entitled to fire back. Four ATF agents were killed in the confusion, and according to the Waco newspaper's reconstruction, at least two of them were probably killed by fire from other agents.

With that, the great testosterone contest began. Hundreds of law enforcement agents surrounded the compound for fifty-one days, most of them muttering, "He can't get away with this," "We'll show him," and other variations on "My dick is bigger than his dick." Meanwhile, there's Koresh inside, just as gooney as a natural-born idiot, under the happy impression that he's chatting with God.

Not only was there no reason to attack the compound fifty-one days ago, there was no reason to attack it yesterday either. Dick DeGuerin, Koresh's lawyer, was obviously still in shock yesterday afternoon. He said, "Oh yeah, of course he would have come out peacefully. We've got it in writing from him. He wanted to finish working on this manuscript. If they had asked Jack or me, we could have told them, 'Everything is peaceful in there.' But these people just kept escalating the hostilities."

All kinds of folks are now claiming knowledgeably, "He never would have come out of there. He wanted to die and take the rest of them with him." I don't know what makes them so certain. At least DeGuerin had actually talked to Koresh.

DeGuerin said, "I was over at Rex Cauble's trial this mornin' and when I heard, when I saw what they were doing, using those Bradleys to push over the walls and gassing those kids, I asked the judge to let me out of the trial. I came straight here. Those Bradleys were tearing apart the kids' rooms. I saw those kids in their rooms. They were peaceful and happy." DeGuerin's voice wobbled badly. "All they were doing was reading the Bible."

The proximate cause for the second raid on the Koresh compound was not tactics or strategy, as the FBI so solemnly reported to Janet Reno. It was the FBI's fear of looking ridiculous. "We're startin' to look silly" was the mutter outside the compound for the last week, and indeed, the stand-off had become fodder for late-night comics. Why should seventeen children die because some tough laws were afraid of looking silly? No one has a right to put ridicule ahead of children's lives.

Maybe Koresh wouldn't've come out after he finished his manuscript. So what? They'd already thrown a fence around the place. All they had to do was post one guard at the gate. Who needed the million-dollar-a-day operation with the choppers and the M-60's? "They could be in there for months," said the alarmists. And who would that have hurt?

The hopelessly provincial Washington press corps is now trying to make this into a Washington story: The blame game is on, fingers pointing, accusations flying. Attorney General Reno is a stand-up gal. Bill Clinton is hiding behind her skirts.

Will the FBI director be fired over this? Who in Washington should get the blame?

No one. This deal had dog-all to do with Washington. It was a machismo contest in Waco between a lot of big, tough law guys and a nut who didn't even know he was in a contest.

But they got a hell of an ending for their made-for-TV movies, didn't they? I do hope the people in Waco in charge of the operation get a lot of money for their exclusive stories.

Fort Worth Star-Telegram, April 20, 1993

OF HOG HUNTS AND
HUMANKIND

We had some big excitement in my neighborhood on Thursday. For reasons too complicated to explain, there was a camera crew from New York in my house filming old boots. I was settin' in the study reading about the civil war between the fundamentalists and the professional educators in Hawkins County, Tennessee, when the sound person rushed in and said, "There's a biiiig pig in the street!"

Well, you never know what a person from New York will consider a big pig, but I wandered out to take a look-see and sure as a by-God, there was a boar hog standin' in the middle of Alta Vista Avenue in south Austin, Texas. Despite what you may have heard about south Austin, hogs are not common in the streets here.

The neighbors were all piling out to inspect the beast with wonder: He was a particularly hairy specimen. I live in a neighborhood that used to be just small wood and brick houses. It was a working-class neighborhood with some low-rent apart-

335

ments at one end of the block and a semimansion that's actually on the Historic Register at the other end. In between, the place is getting to be fairly yuppified. The more avant-garde neighbors have taken up xeriscaping; the hog snuffled off into a xeriscape but didn't care for the cactus and snuffled out again.

By this time, the assembled neighbors and camera crew had been joined by an astonished motorist, who brought his van to a dead halt while his kids hung out the windows and shrieked at the hog.

Since we were Texans all, save the New Yorkers, naturally someone yelled, "Git a rope!" I fetched a rope from the pickup and the guy driving the camera crew volunteered to lasso the brute, having, he said, some rodeo experience. The hog objected to this program and headed up into the Hopkinses' yard. Mr. Hopkins, who is eighty-some and spends a fair amount of time napping on his front porch, came to, and started waving his arms and hollering, "Shoo, hog! Shoo, hog!" The hog headed for the Hopkinses' hydrangeas with the full posse in pursuit, all givin' directions to one another about the best way to lasso a hog. For some reason, Mr. Hopkins got to laughing.

I'll say this for New Yorkers — they're gamers. They trailed that hog up the street, more cars screechin', more kids yellin'.

I go back to the house to phone the city's animal-control folks and wind up talkin' to a lady who sounds like Lily Tomlin doin' Ernestine.

"And whose pet pig is it?" she inquired nasally.

"Lady, this is not anybody's pet pot-bellied pig. We're lookin' at a hundred-fifty, maybe two hundred pounds of boar hog out here."

"We've had several cases of those pot-bellied pigs getting out," she replied through her nose. "Are you sure one of the neighbors isn't keeping a little pig in the house?"

Meanwhile, the hog and posse come loping back down the block.

I'm still arguing with Ernestine, who now wants to know my home phone number, blood type, and mother's maiden name because she has to fill out a form. Outside, the whole gang reappears in my front window going the other direction, like a scene in a Mack Sennett comedy. The hog is doing some great broken-field running. The lighting guy with the ponytail gets a hand on the hog, and the producer stands in front of it waving her arms and yells, "Stop! You're under arrest!" The carpenter who was working at Joe and Mary's next door tries a tackle but the hog breaks clear and they all disappear up the block again. Ernestine says, "And your Social Security number?"

I go out to rejoin the posse and we all pursue the hog, yippin' and hollerin' after this miscreant swine. We chase it up one hill, down another, back up and into the brush behind the apartments, where we lost him. The kids continued to search the woods, looking for the spoor of the beast for another half hour, while the grown-ups stood around discussing the strategy of the hunt. It was generally agreed none of us had had so much fun in ages. By sundown, the hog hunt had already achieved the status of block mythology, the hog got bigger with every retelling, and those neighbors coming home from work mourned missing all the fun.

I went back to reading about this terrible situation in Tennessee, where some folks became convinced their neighbors were Satanists and Lord knows what-all, on account of the fundamentalists didn't like a story about Martians in a schoolbook. Such a knot of religious intolerance, conspiracy theories, and lawsuits you never heard tell of — it just split that whole community to bits. I got to thinking about the variety of humanity that had just engaged in the Great Alta Vista Hog Hunt — the guy from New York with an earring, the rodeo roper, Mr. Hopkins. Maybe we should let more hogs loose in this country. Isn't that how mankind learned to cooperate in the first place — by joining in the hunt? We could just focus more on cooperation instead of concentrating on our differences. Chasing hogs is more fun, though.

Fort Worth Star-Telegram, May 2, 1993

ON WHY WE LOVED KUGLE

Bill Kugle of Athens has gone and died, leaving us shy of probably the most fun-loving freedom-fighter Texas ever produced.

What a fighter and a lover was Kugle. What a glorious, joyous, life-embracing, Constitution-loving, laff riot of a life he led. He fought, sequentially, the Japanese in the Pacific during World War II, the mob in Galveston, the pinheads in the Texas Legislature, racism in East Texas, and sourpusses at all times and on all fronts. He loved running rivers in Texas, riding motorcycles in Mexico, freedom, justice, his kids, several wives and women in general, country music, beer, food, camping, and people.

He was sixty-seven when he died, watching the Dallas Cowboys win a game — perfect. They'd been begging him to slow down since the first heart attack over a year earlier. Even Ann Richards, whom Kugle adored, wrote him, called him, pleaded — "But what's a mother to do?" she recalled at his memorial service in Austin. You couldn't slow Kugle down any more than you can catch a rainbow: He was always at full throttle, with the enthusiasm of an eight-year-old boy.

There are so many great Kugle stories, but let's start in the Lege. It's 1953, and Kugle, a young lawyer out of Galveston, is one of a handful of members to stand and oppose a resolution inviting Senator Joseph McCarthy to address a joint session of the Texas Legislature. At the back mike he said, "Members. I just want you to consider one thing. As many of you know, by the time I was twenty I had been a paratrooper for three years [according to his service buddies, Kugle had done quite a bit of hand-to-hand fighting]. And I swear this to you: If that man [McCarthy] walks through those doors [right behind him], it will be. Over. My. Dead. Body." And then he sat down.

Of course the resolution carried anyway: Fortunately, McCarthy was too busy to come. Kugie was also offered a bribe that session: It came from the Maceo brothers, the mobsters who then ruled Galveston. They actually tried to bribe him twice: the D.A. wouldn't act on it the first time Kugle reported it; the second time, Kugle taped it. The D.A. indicted the man who had offered the money, but alas, the fellow decided to go swimming while full of gunshot holes and with a large chunk of cement around his feet. Kugle slept with a shotgun under his bed for two years.

He moved on to East Texas, and I wish you could have seen the memorial service in Athens: has to have been the best integrated gathering in East Texas in years. Kugle spent so long organizing voters around Athens that some of his precinct captains changed from father to son or from father to daughter. Judge Neil Caldwell of Alvin believes the happiest he ever saw Kugle was one day in Mexico City when Kugle let out a whoop that stopped traffic for a block in every direction, started whirling around in a mad Indian-dance hop, hooting and flapping his arms: He had just learned from an English-language paper that that sorry s.o.b. Congressman John Dowdy had finally gotten himself indicted.

In addition to his law practice and political work, Kugle carried on an extensive correspondence. One set of letters, which has shown up on law school bulletin boards around Texas for years, was occasioned by the death of a bull owned by C. B. Welborn, which drowned in a cesspool due to the alleged carelessness of some city workers of Trinidad, a town represented by Kugle. Kugle's stately response to the first unpleasant intimation of legal action by Welborn reads: "It is with heavy heart that I endeavor to compose an appropriate response to your communication which brought to the Mayor and me intelligence of a profound tragedy occurring on the periphery of our lives. It is certainly inadequate to say that we were saddened by the knowledge of the death of Mr. Welborn's bull. The tragedy is compounded by your advice that the deceased was destined to become, in your words, 'the herd bull.' Many are called, but few are chosen. Becoming a herd bull is a status to which I might have aspired in my youth, but such hopes are usually so visionary and fanciful. That Mr. Welborn's dead bull had it made, in a manner of speaking, but yet never knew fulfillment because he was struck down in the morn of life, fills one with frustration at understanding the injustices which fate so capriciously lays upon us." After much more flowery prose, he continued: "Mayor Miller and I have in concert searched the corporate conscience of the city of Trinidad in a dedicated effort to divine whether any responsibility for the death of Welborn's bull lay with the city. We cannot but conclude that Welborn's bull met his death by reason of his own predeliction for mischief and, accordingly, deny liability in the premises."

That this was not Kugle's natural style is shown by a brief epistle to some moronic school board member: "Dear Mr. Gregg, Your vote to purge Darwin from biology textbooks is the greatest accolade for ignorance since the trial of Galileo. Sincerely," etc.

Kugle's friend Jack Skaggs, a South Texas lawyer, once wrote to him: "I also thought you might be interested in the enclosed verdict that I got last week in Brownsville in a medical malpractice case. My client had lost three centimeters from the length of his male organ during a botched urethroplasty which was performed to remove a urethral stricture. I have always wondered the exact value of this apparatus in dollars and cents. We now know that on the border at least, it is worth $270,000 per centimeter. Would the price be more or less in East Texas?"

Kugle replied, "I don't know what the value would be in East Texas, but if it happened to me it would be a sex-change operation."

Another one-sentence letter went to Senator Lloyd Bentsen on October 5, 1987: "Re: Bork nomination. Dear Senator Bentsen, I will always be your friend. Bill Kugle."

There being no delicate way to put this, I suppose I should just come right out and say that Kugle was a shameless pussyhound. They played "Your Cheatin' Heart" at his memorial service, which touched off some unseemly giggling. But all his wives came, fond of him to the end: I never knew anyone who knew him who wasn't. Ann Richards said at the service that Kugle liked risk, liked putting himself totally into whatever he was doing — running rivers or working for Ralph Yarborough, risking death or heartbreak, because it made life and victory so much sweeter. I don't know if he liked risk or it was just his nature to live everything with more passion and more energy than most of us. He kept it all right to the end: He was undiminished, unfatigued by life. He had such zest for it all, he relished it so.

We'll put up many a merry fight in your memory, Kugie.

June 1993

THE SEVENTY-THIRD SESSION

The seventy-third session of the Texas Legislature is pretty much typified by the following Warren Chisum story, Chisum being the Bible-thumping dwarf from Pampa who has added such je ne sais quoi to the proceedings this year.

The Texas Senate had a rare moment of courage and voted to remove homosexual sodomy from the revised version of the penal code. All were astonished. The revision made its way over to the House, where Representative Chisum promptly rose and introduced an amendment to reinstate the damn thing. The Housies were afraid everyone would think they were queer if they didn't vote for it, so they did. Then some scholar explains to Chisum that unless he reinstates heterosexual sodomy as well, it's going to be declared unconstitutional. So Chisum promptly rises and moves to do that.

Whereupon we had one of the more bizarre debates in the history of the Lege, with assorted avant-garde members rising at the back mike to say approximately, "Uh, Warren, suppose I am in bed with my lawfully wedded spouse and I, like, kind of mis-aim and wind up in the wrong hole. You don't want to send to me to prison for that, do you?"

Chisum would stoutly reply, "Yes, I do. It's against nature and the Bible." So the Housies were afraid everyone would think they were perverts if they didn't vote it, so they did. Chisum then shook hands with his ally Talmadge Heflin of Houston in celebration of this double triumph, and the Speaker had to send the sergeant at arms over to reprimand them both. Because under Chisum's own amendments, it's illegal for a prick to touch an asshole in this state.

On the other major burning issue of the session, let me say now — I was wrong. I thought the concealed-handgun bill was the dumbest thing the Lege had done since the dildo law and said so at length and vociferously. I have changed my mind. I now believe Texans should have the right to carry concealed weapons. I just want to add one amendment: Everyone who carries a concealed weapon is required to wear a beanie with a propeller on top.

The Legislature increased spending on education by 3.6 percent, which will not even cover increased enrollment, but we increased prison spending by 37 percent. That's on top of the $2.5 billion we have spent building new prisons since 1988. No one is feeling safer.

Our other big news is that John Connally has died. *De mortuis nil nisi bonum* and all that, but there has been an awful lot of hagiographic slop printed about Connally. In fact, he was a good governor for Texas: His enduring legacy to the state is a system of higher education that sometimes threatens to become first-rate and is still cheap. And he raised the taxes to pay for it too. For that he deserves much credit. Believe me, we've had governors who never achieved anything at all.

But Ronnie Dugger used to say, "John Connally never messes with the topwaters." The topwaters are the little fish that swim on the top of the pond: Connally liked to deal with the big fish, the ones with money and power that swim deep. One of the most telling examples I know of came in the summer of 1966, when a raggle-taggle march of farm workers started out from the Rio Grande Valley on the Fourth of July. This was no union movement, no César Chavez deal — they were led by local priests and they wanted to walk to Austin to present a petition to the governor on Labor Day, just present a petition asking for an increase in the state minimum wage. State minimum was twenty-five cents an hour, for stoop labor in the valley sun.

Took them almost two months to get near Austin. Some folks had set dogs on them along the way, others let them drink out of the garden hose. Two days before Labor Day, John Connally drove out to meet them in an air-conditioned Lincoln, accompanied by Attorney General Waggoner Carr and Ben Barnes. Connally got out of the Lincoln, shook a few hands, congratulated the marchers on their "orderliness," and then announced he wouldn't be in Austin on Labor Day to receive their petition because it was the start of dove-hunting season. He shook a few more hands, then got back into his air-conditioned Lincoln and drove off, leaving the marchers in the dust by the side of the road.

July 1993

THE FUN'S IN THE FIGHT

I've been talkin' to a bunch of the fun-lovin' freedom fighters of Texas lately, and we all agree that there's one thing we need to pass on to all of y'all from the few of us before I take a leave from these pages. (I'm takin' a leave of absence on account of I have to write a book, and time has become both scant and precious.) The thing is this: You got to have fun while you're fightin' for freedom, 'cause you don't always win.

Havin' fun while freedom fightin' must be one of those lunatic Texas traits we get from the water — which is known to have lithium in it — because it goes all the way back to Sam Houston, surely the most lovable, the most human, and the funniest of all the Great Men this country has ever produced. While Sam was president of the Republic of Texas, he was visited by a French ambassador. This Frog was quite the wonder of frontier Austin; he minced along the wooden sidewalks wearing a silk suit with lace at the collar and cuffs, with a gilt épée, no less, slung along his side. Though Sam had a perfectly good fine house, he elected to receive the Frenchman in a log hut with a mud floor. By choice a sometime Indian, Sam wore only fringed leggings and a blanket around his big ol' hairy chest.

While the French ambassador held forth grandiloquently, Houston, who was himself a magnificent orator, replied only with an occasional, "Ugh."

Our Texas freedom fighters have been prone to misbehavior ever since. A recent Ku Klux Klan rally in Austin produced an eccentric counterdemonstration. When the fifty Klansmen appeared (they were bused in from Waco) in front of the state capitol, they were greeted by five thousand locals who had turned out for a "Moon the Klan" rally. Citizens dropped trou both singly and in groups, occasionally producing a splendid wave effect. It was a swell do.

But I reckon the man who taught most of us how to have fun while fightin' for freedom was John Henry Faulk, who went and died on us a few years back. Despite gettin' blacklisted during the McCarthy era and having a number of other misadventures during his life, Johnny never lost his sense of mischief, and to the end of his days, he could be counted on to hatch some elaborate practical joke to bedevil whichever do-badder had most recently and most egregiously harmed the cause of liberty and justice for all.

Johnny used to tell a story about when he was a Texas Ranger, a captain in fact. He was seven at the time. His friend Boots Cooper, who was six, was sheriff, and the two of them used to do

349

a lot of heavy law enforcement out behind the Faulk place in south Austin. One day Johnny's mama, having two such fine officers on the place, asked them to go down to the hen house and rout out the chicken snake that had been doing some damage there.

Johnny and Boots loped down to the hen house on their trusty brooms (which they tethered outside) and commenced to search for the snake. They went all through the nests on the bottom shelf of the hen house and couldn't find it, so the both of them stood on tippy-toes to look on the top shelf. I myself have never been nose-to-nose with a chicken snake, but I always took Johnny's word for it that it will just scare the living shit out of you. Scared those boys so bad that they both tried to exit the hen house at the same time, doing considerable damage to both themselves and the door.

Johnny's mama, Miz Faulk, was a kindly lady, but watching all this, it struck her funny. She was still laughin' when the captain and the sheriff trailed back up to the front porch. "Boys, boys," said Miz Faulk, "what is wrong with you? You know perfectly well a chicken snake cannot hurt you."

That's when Boots Cooper made his semi-immortal observation. "Yes ma'am," he said, "but there's some things'll scare you so bad, you hurt yourself."

And isn't that what we keep doing in this country, over and over again? We get scared so bad — about the communist menace or illegal immigration or AIDS or pornography or violent crime, some damn scary thing — that we hurt ourselves. We take the odd notion that the only way to protect ourselves is to give up some of our freedom — just trim a little, hedge a bit, and we'll all be safe after all.

Those who think of freedom in this country as one long, broad path leading ever onward and up- ward are dead damned wrong. Many a time free- dom has been rolled back — and always for the same sorry reason: fear.

So one thing I have learned from Johnny Faulk, Texas, and life, is that since you don't always win, you got to learn to enjoy just fightin' the good fight.

On the occasion of the bicentennial of the Con- stitution, the ACLU was fixin' to lay some heavy lifetime freedom-fighter awards on various citi- zens, and one of 'em was Joe Rauh, the lawyer who defended so many folks during the McCarthy era and the civil rights movement (note that the rightness of those stands is always easier to see in retrospect). Rauh was sick in the hospital at the time and asked a friend of his to go down and collect the award for him. His friend went to see him in the hospital and said, "Joe, what you want me to tell these folks?"

So there was Rauh lyin' there sick as a dog, thinkin' back on all those bad, ugly, angry times — the destroyed careers, the wrecked lives — and he said, "Tell 'em how much fun it was. Tell 'em how much fun it was."

351

So keep fightin' for freedom and justice, beloveds, but don't you forget to have fun doin' it. Lord, let your laughter ring forth. Be outrageous, ridicule the fraidy-cats, rejoice in all the oddities that freedom can produce. And when you get through kickin' ass and celebratin' the sheer joy of a good fight, be sure to tell those who come after how much fun it was.

Mother Jones, May/June 1993